ACKNOWLEDGEMENTS

Many thanks for assistance with this new edition go out to:

William P. Carl, for the many hours he spent revising the "Artists in Dealer Catalogs" section and his original contribution of the current text .

Cynthia Tukis, for her expertise and valuable assistance in editing and preparation of the final copy of the text.

James R. Bakker Antiques, Inc., Skinner, Inc., and the Morisi Ortiz Family Trust for providing many of the photographs in this *Guide*.

Nora Pires, for the many hours spent compiling and revising the thousands of prices which make up this *Guide*.

My parents, Lillian and William, for their encouragement and support - as always.

My wife, Donna, her mother, Lorraine, my daughter,Danielle, and my son, Christopher, who from the beginning, all supported me, encouraged me, and showed, most of all, understanding. I thank you especially, with love.

William T. Currier

D0291537

Currier's Price Guide to AMERICAN and EUROPEAN PRINTS at AUCTION

Current Price Ranges on the Original Prints of
Over 2600 American and European Artists at Auction

THIRD EDITION

text written by William P. Carl
prices edited by William P. Carl and William T. Currier

CURRIER
PUBLICATIONS

ISBN   0-935277-19-6 Softcover
Library of Congress
Catalog Card Number 94-70933

Printed in the United States of America

COVER PHOTO:

Afternoon Swimming, **David Hockney**, Color lithograph, Edition 55, 1979, 31 1/2" x 39 1/2", Courtesy of Sotheby's, Inc.,New York, NY

Additional copies of this book may be obtained from bookstores and selected antique dealers. To order directly from the publisher, remit $18.95 per copy, plus $3.00 shipping and handling (book rate), or $4.00 (first class). MA addresses add 5% sales tax. For bulk order discounts (6 or more copies) please write, or call, for details to:

CURRIER PUBLICATIONS
241 Main Street
Stoneham, MA 02180 (800) 344-0760

[Make check or money order payable to CURRIER PUBLICATIONS]
(U.S. dollars only, please)

Dedicated to all our valued customers.

About the Author

William P. Carl

A dealer in fine original prints in Boston, Massachusetts since 1976, William P. Carl is a well-known expert in the field. His academic background includes a Bachelor of Arts degree from Colgate University and a Master of Science degree in library science from Simmons College. He has worked as a curatorial assistant in the Wiggin Print Room of the Boston Public Library and from 1976-1982 he was head of the print department of Childs Gallery, Boston. Mr. Carl has served as an advisor to museums and private collectors and has organized innumerable exhibitions. He is also a member of the International Fine Print Dealers Association (I.F.P.D.A.).

Of special note is William P. Carl's own artistic ability. For the past several years he has specialized in producing color woodcuts, and to his credit the Boston Public Library, the National Museum of American Art in Washington, as well as several notable private collectors have acquired his work. He is presently represented by the Annex Galleries in Santa Rosa, California.

Mr. Carl can be reached in Boston by writing to Post Office Box 67178, Chestnut Hill, MA 02167 or telephoning him at (617) 277-9135.

TABLE OF CONTENTS

CHAPTER TWO

Using This Guide

Fine Art Prints at Auction

Artists in Dealer Catalogs

APPENDIX

PREFACE

Until the author, William P. Carl, provided the information for this *Guide*, there was no other practical reference available in an inexpensive, compact, concise and easy to carry format that could help quickly assess the potential worth of fine examples of American and European prints, from the 16th century to the present. It will be invaluable to: antique dealers, auctioneers, print collectors, estate lawyers, bank trust officers, art consultants, appraisers, and print dealers. *Currier's Price Guide to American and European Prints at Auction* may well be the most profitable investment that anyone, who has occasion to buy and sell fine art prints, could ever make.

You will find that you have purchased the most practical price guide to 500 years of American and European prints available today. The compilation of data here will be useful to even the most seasoned veteran:

▶ Accurate spellings of artists' names.

▶ Accurate birth and death dates not easily found elsewhere.

▶ Price ranges for as many as three printing techniques for each of the over 2,600 artists listed.

▶ A "special" list of over 425 artists who appear frequently in dealer catalogs nationally, with the price ranges for their work.

▶ An appendix containing public and private institutions for research, auction houses selling prints, and an extensive bibliography for further reading.

There are many instances which can be sighted where this *Guide* will prove invaluable. Some examples follow.

Auctioneers can use the price ranges to help establish a starting bid on prints by artists with whom they are unfamiliar, or help screen prints for possible consignment.

Print collectors will find the *Guide* extremely interesting and especially helpful when hunting for artists whose work falls only within certain price ranges (e.g., $400-$7,500) and/or who specialize in certain printing techniques (e.g., relief, intaglio, etc.). Many collectors will want to carry a copy with them as they frequent yard sales, flea markets, thrift shops, or country auctions. Not infrequently, many "sleepers" can be uncovered.

Appraisers can use the *Guide* to quickly find what the highest price realized at auction has been on a particular artist's work. They can use this information as a starting point, then proceed to do further research on the actual auction results.

Because of information gleaned from our *Guide*, many estate executors may want to pursue a professional appraisal on certain prints. It would not be unusual for someone running an estate "tag sale" to price something well below its true market value.

Antique dealers, who have occasion to buy and sell prints, but who have very little knowledge of the print market will find our *Guide* to be one of the most important reference books in their library. The *Guide* will help many dealers to avoid the problem of buying too high or selling too low. And help them to *quickly* assess the *potential* value of prints in many situations: house calls, estate sales, etc. Dealers can quickly determine if a recent purchase needs more research before pricing it for resale.

Add to the list, the many thrift shop owners, pickers, museum personnel, art framers, and yard sale and flea market fanatics who will find our *Guide* useful; and you can only agree that *Currier's Price Guide to American and European Prints at Auction* is the first place to look for values on the works of over 2,600 artists worldwide.

One final note: You are welcome and encouraged to comment, and feel free to suggest changes or additions which will improve this *Guide*. Please write or call:

CURRIER PUBLICATIONS
241 Main Street
Stoneham, MA 02180
(800) 344-0760

CHAPTER ONE

Pricing Your Print

Purpose and Focus

The purpose of this *Guide* is to assist you in determining the value of a particular work of graphic art. This is not necessarily a quick and easy matter, as most of you probably realize. The field of original prints is complex, diverse and prone to all sorts of exceptions. Nonetheless, what we attempt to provide here, for the novice, is a starting point for further research and discovery. We are here to help you assess the *potential* value of your original prints, whatever they might be: good or bad, major or minor, old or not so old.

The focus of this *Guide* is the "fine art print." Broadly speaking, this refers to an original work of art produced from a matrix: a plate, block, stone or other such surface on which the artist *himself* has created an image. Every impression, or print, taken from this printing surface is an original work of art. The fact that more than one impression exists does not in any way lessen the merits of an artist's prints. Some artists simply choose printmaking over painting, drawing or sculpturing as a means to express their ideas at a particular moment. According to some art critics, many artists over the centuries produced their best work in fine prints - prints that they, themselves, created.

Printmaking Techniques

The fine prints of which we speak are most often produced by one of three basic techniques: relief, intaglio, and planographic. Nearly all forms of original graphic art will fit into one of these three categories. There are mixed media prints which can be quite complex but, for the purpose of this *Guide*, it will suffice to briefly describe the three working techniques. You should consult the bibliography at the end of this *Guide* for further information on the specific techniques of printmaking.

RELIEF

The relief technique, which is the oldest and most basic method of making original prints, encompasses woodcuts, linoleum cuts, metal cuts and wood engravings. Basically, a design is drawn on the surface of a block and the area around the design is cut away. The surface in relief is inked and then printed.

Albrecht Durer (1471-1528) used this technique with outstanding success in his woodcuts; the German Expressionist printmakers, among them Kirchner, Heckel, and Nolde, produced creative results with this technique during the first half of the twentieth century; and many contemporary artists are using it today.

Here are four examples of relief prints.

Dory Fishermen
by Tod Lindenmuth, color linocut
(Courtesy of James R. Bakker Antiques, Inc., Cambridge, MA)

Torcello,
by Margaret J. Patterson, color wooblock
(Courtesy of James R. Bakker Antiques, Inc., Cambridge, MA)

The Convalescent
by Eliza D. Gardiner, color woodblock
(Courtesy of a Private Collection)

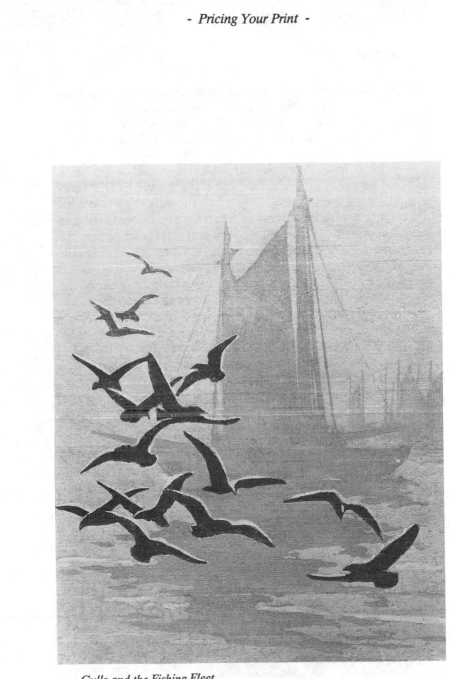

Gulls and the Fishing Fleet
by Tod Lindenmuth, color linocut
(Courtesy of James R. Bakker Antiques, Inc., Cambridge, MA)

INTAGLIO

The second basic technique of printmaking, intaglio, encompasses a variety of individual processes, such as, etching, drypoint, mezzotint, aquatint and soft-ground etching. Each can achieve quite different artistic expressions and can be used in combination or separately.

Intaglio, basically, employs an etched or incised design which is *below* the surface of the plate. In effect, it is the reverse of the relief technique. Acid is used to etch ("bite") into the plate or an engraving tool is employed to make an incision. Then the incised or etched area is inked and printed. The pressure of the press and plate against the paper results in a noticeable depression surrounding the border of the image. This depression mark is called the *platemark*.

The variety of effects that can be achieved is one of the strengths of this technique. Rembrandt, Goya and Picasso, for example, all used intaglio printmaking with success but their work side by side looks quite different. Although intaglio is a centuries old technique it is still being used today with great success.

Here are four examples of intaglio prints.

Morning, 1915
by Frank Weston Benson, drypoint
(Courtesy of Skinner, Inc., Bolton, MA)

Geometric Abstractions
by Sonia Terk Delauney, color etching
(Courtesy of Skinner, Inc, Bolton, MA)

La Main, 1966
by Antonio Clave, aquatint
(Courtesy of James R. Bakker Antiques, Inc., Cambridge, MA)

Self Portrait, 1906
by Anders Leonard Zorn, etching
(Courtesy of James R. Bakker Antiques, Inc., Cambridge, MA)

PLANOGRAPHIC

The third technique of printmaking is the planographic or surface technique, otherwise referred to as lithography. This late 18th century invention first flourished in western Europe and later in America. Unlike the relief or intaglio techniques, in lithography the design is drawn on a porous limestone or specially treated metal plate with a grease crayon. The design is then "fixed" to the surface to prevent the image from spreading. Water is then applied to the entire surface, followed by an application of ink. The greasy part of the surface - the design or image - attracts the ink, and the wet surface repels it. This inked design or image can then be run through a specially designed press from which the ink is transferred to a sheet of paper.

Lithographic printing is traditionally a complicated process and usually requires a professional printer to achieve the finest results. Unlike other graphic techniques, with this process there is the potential for producing very large editions (i.e., the total number of impressions) since the design on the stone and the stone itself do not easily wear down.

Here are three examples of planographic prints (all lithographs).

Westmorland Entrance
by Joseph Jones, lithograph
(Courtesy of James R. Bakker Antiques, Inc., Cambridge, MA)

Abstract Figures
by Wilfredo Lam, lithograph
(Courtesy of James R. Bakker Antiques, Inc., Cambridge, MA)

Honorary Degree, 1937
by Grant Wood, lithograph
(Courtesy of James R. Bakker Antiques, Inc., Cambridge, MA)

Please note: For the purpose of this Guide, the stencil and monotype process will be included under the planographic technique. A brief description of each follows:

Stencil

The stencil process, more commonly known today as silk-screen or serigraph, is a twentieth century innovation which first flourished in this country during the 1930's and 1940's in conjunction with the Federal Art Project in New York. Artists in France and England also employed this process during the first half of the century. The process is simple, requiring the artist to cut out a stencil through which pigment is squeegeed and an exact replica of the design appears on the paper. Silk is introduced as a supporting element to make printing easier and allow for more intricate design work. As the process became more sophisticated over the years, the cut stencil approach was superseded by the tusche washout method which is a bit more complicated.

The advantages of the silk-screen process are that it does not require a printing press and is well suited to designs which have broad areas of bold, flat colors. The disadvantage of this process is that the surface of a silk-screen print is easily damaged, as abrasions and cracks can appear quickly without proper handling. A detailed discussion of condition as it relates to prints and their value is addressed later in this text.

Monotype

The monotype process is an exciting and distinctive approach to making original prints, dating as far back as the 17th century. It flourished in the hands of Degas in the late 19th century, and today continues to be an improvisational and creative technique among contemporary printmakers.

The monotype process involves making a design with a quick-drying pigment on a flat surface, often a copperplate, and running it through a press. The resultant print is a unique work of art which generally cannot be printed in multiples, unlike the other techniques which we discussed earlier. With this technique, if the same plate is run through the press again, the image will be much lighter and different in effect. Degas very successfully explored this concept and produced unique, but similar, multiple prints. As a general statement about monotypes, these uncommon prints have a very "painterly" look about them and brushwork is usually quite evident on the surface. Like etchings, monotypes *do* have a platemark as a means to identify them; lithographs do not.

Here are examples of a silkscreen and monotype print.

Petunias, 1943
by Blanche Lazzell, color monotype
(Courtesy of Skinner, Inc., Bolton, MA)

Susan, 1976
by Alex Katz, silkscreen
(Courtesy of Skinner, Inc., Bolton, MA)

Factors Which Determine Value

One of the most perplexing and ongoing issues is that of assessing the value of a particular original print, whether it is an etching, woodcut, lithograph, etc. Why is *this* Rembrandt etching worth more than *that* Rembrandt etching? Why does a tear in the image of *that* Whistler print make it worth so much less than another in fine condition? Why is *my* Durer print so close in many details to the one in the museum collection but still mine has no value as a photogravure? These are some of the questions which come to mind as we begin our discussion of values and relative values in the marketplace of fine prints.

NAME

First of all, the name of the artist is a key factor affecting the value of an original print. Who did it? That's the question which everyone asks first. Fortunately, most fine prints are signed; even most early engravings and etchings, e.g., those done during the time of Durer (16th Century), are signed in some way if only with a monogram; hence, the problem of dubious authorship which negatively affects the value of so many paintings and drawings is not as much a factor with prints.

So what's in a name? - quite a bit, unfortunately. There are innumerable lesser known artists who created beautiful prints and because of their lack of renown, they sell for less than what logic might suggest. Conversely, there are many well-known artists, particularly painters who also made prints, and their work sells for more than one would expect - even if the prints themselves are not particularly fine. Renoir, for one, who was primarily a painter, also produced graphic works which are of questionable quality; but the prints command a high price relative to a lot of other lesser known artists.

CONDITION

The question of condition is an important one, in fact, far more important than many people realize. Prints which have serious condition problems are indeed worth far less than impressions of the same print in fine condition. A tear into the image, faded colors, abrasions on the surface of the print, insoluble stains and other extreme condition problems are relevant issues which negatively affect the value of a particular print. These are problems which cannot really be undone. A tear is a tear is a tear. Even if it is skillfully repaired by a professional paper conservator, the problem will continue to haunt the print for the rest of its life. The same permanency applies to faded colors.

Once a color print has been faded by over-exposure to sunlight (and this takes a long time), the damage is permanent. Hand-colored prints can be retouched with success but, nonetheless, the original stature of the print has been altered. This is true for printed colors as well. Many color woodcuts and color lithographs from the last hundred years have been affected by sunlight. The differences can be subtle or drastic since certain inks and certain colors are more susceptible to fading than others. To determine the extent of the fading it is important to do a comparative study by locating another impression and placing it side by side with the one you have. This takes time and effort but it is all part of assessing the value of an original print.

Surface abrasions are like tears - they will always be there. A scrape in the image can be "touched in" by a professional conservator but the problem remains. A print may look fine but closer scrutiny can often reveal a world of hidden problems. In fact, some repairs are so good they are not at all easy to spot. This is something to watch for at all times, particularly with old master prints where old, clever repair work has had time to age with the rest of the print.

There are other less serious condition problems such as foxing, small tears in the outer margins, old and improper hinges at the top of the sheet, and mat stains from an earlier acidic mat. These problems can, for the most part, be undone. A professional paper conservator can rescue a print in a sickly state and revive it to make it stable, presentable and ultimately more salable. It is important that beginning collectors realize that condition problems can be critical and some are more serious than others. Sensitivity to such matters comes about only with experience looking at prints of all kinds. A bad tear or stain will cut the value of a print sometimes in half, or even more, depending on the severity of the damage. There is no steadfast rule regarding how much condition affects value but always keep it in mind when buying. *If something appears especially cheap there just might be a good reason for it.*

QUALITY OF IMPRESSION

Quality of impression is another factor which affects the value of an original print. This is especially true with old master prints since printing presses were not as sophisticated and there was no established concept of the limited edition. During the early years of printmaking, the sixteenth to eighteenth centuries, prints were printed, for the most part, as they were needed. If a particular image was popular, then more and more impressions were printed from the copperplate or the woodblock. The problem with this is that after awhile the printing surface changes, so that one can begin to see a dramatic transformation as more and more impressions come off the press. This is particularly true with popular artists, such as, Rembrandt and Durer, whose prints were sought after early on and most extant impressions of their prints were actually printed after the artists were deceased.

Durer did not destroy his woodblocks after printing, nor did Rembrandt cancel out his copperplates. Many of their plates and blocks were passed on over the years (as with other artists) and certain individuals even re-worked many of the Rembrandt plates in an attempt to restore the qualities which were lost due to wear and tear and excessive printing. The results were usually not very successful but they *can* be very tricky and that's where further research and comparative study come into play.

The delicate richness of drypoint in a Rembrandt landscape etching is lost very quickly in the printing process, and a late impression of a Durer woodcut has breaks in the lines and lacks the clarity and sharpness of an early printing. For the untrained eye, the best way to ascertain the overall quality of the impression in question is to compare it with another good impression, preferably one in a reputable museum collection. In addition, a knowledgeable dealer, or the print specialist at an auction house, can be very helpful and informative. Only with this kind of effort can you begin to learn the subtleties of impressions and just how much they can vary.

The extent to which the quality of an impression affects the value of a print is no better illustrated than with the prints of Rembrandt (1606-1669). During the 1988 auction season, for example, there were ten impressions of the portrait etching, "Jan Lutma, Goldsmith," up for sale among the major auction houses. The range of prices realized varied from $960 to $506,000!

This is a fairly extreme case but it is not uncommon to have an enormous variation in value between a poor impression and a brilliant impression. Condition, of course, is always a factor but never underestimate the importance of impression quality. Just because someone tells you he owns an original Rembrandt does not necessarily mean a great deal. It may be a late, washed out, reworked impression of a common print. It could also be a superb, rich early impression of a rare and desirable subject, worth $200,000 - the differences are that extreme.

Additional Factors Affecting Value

In addition to name, condition and quality of impression, there are many other factors which can affect the value of a print to one degree or another. Here are a few more points to keep in mind when looking at a print that you may possibly purchase, whether from a dealer, auction house, or private party.

MARGINS

It is sometimes difficult to ascertain whether or not a print has trimmed margins and, most importantly, whether anything has been cut away from the original design. Most early prints were traditionally trimmed to slightly outside the platemark, which is perfectly acceptable today among collectors, but a print trimmed into the image is worth less than one with even the slightest margins. This is all relative and, unfortunately, there is no precise rule of thumb regarding prints cut into the image and the subsequent loss of value. It is, nevertheless, something to be aware of particularly with old master prints and large works from all periods. There are many unfortunate cases on record where the prints were cropped here and there to fit a frame!

SIGNATURE

It is important to know just what part an autograph, or lack of one, plays in determining the value of a print. Remember that up to the late 19th century, prints were signed *not* in pencil but rather, only in the plate. A monogram or a last name was etched or engraved into the plate or block as part of the overall design. The hand-signed print, as we know it today, is a fairly recent phenomenon which started to appear in the second half of the 19th century. As time went on, the hand-signed print became more and more a regular part of printmaking, so that today an unsigned work is viewed with some suspicion.

Not all prints were intended to be hand-signed to begin with and this fact does not necessarily detract from their value. The only way to know for sure what you have, signature-wise, is to consult with someone more knowledgeable than yourself. Every artist's work is different. There are always exceptions to the rule and it takes time to learn what to expect when it comes to signatures.

For example, James McNeill Whistler etchings were sometimes signed in the plate with his last name; a few have a "W" only. Some were signed in pencil with a tiny butterfly design (which evolved from the "W") and some were not signed at all. An early Thames work signed in pencil by Whistler is uncommon and worth more because it is not usually encountered. His later Venetian etchings were normally signed with the pencil butterfly design but occasionally an unsigned impression turns up. The unsigned one is worth less than the signed one because the signature is expected to be there. A similar tale of exceptions and contradictions can be told about other artists as well!

Another kind of signature which you encounter on an original print is a stamped facsimile of the artist's written signature. This is an *estate stamp*. It generally means that a particular print by an artist had simply not been pencil signed by the time of that artist's death. The estate stamp "legitimizes" the authorship of the work in question. Most estate stamped prints are, in theory, as desirable as hand signed prints but, as you might suspect, many collectors feel more comfortable with the latter. Consequently, prices between the two can vary. In addition, an unsigned print left behind in the studio raises the question of whether or not the artist ever intended the work to be sold to begin with. This can be difficult to determine and further research may be necessary.

EDITION SIZE

An edition refers to the number of impressions, that is, the number of original prints taken from the block, the lithographic stone or the metal plate. A "small" edition is generally considered fewer than about twenty impressions. A "large" edition consists of more than one hundred and fifty impressions. Some artists printed only a few impressions of a particular image and others printed, perhaps, a thousand or more impressions as part of a portfolio or publication.

Popular artists, such as, Honore Daumier (1808- 1879) and William Hogarth (1697-1764) saw to it that much of their work was widely printed and published and consequently a great many impressions are in circulation today. Other artists, such as, Edgar Degas (1834-1917), printed very small editions and impressions rarely appear on the market today in any form. Even impressions from Degas' cancelled plates can sell for more than $1,000!

Impressions are sometimes taken long after the original edition was printed - even long after the death of the artist. Many of these prints known as restrikes are still in existence. It is often difficult to spot them, since the impressions may be quite good and, to the untrained eye, some restrikes don't appear to be very different from early impressions.

Always remember that an impression printed during the life of the artist is worth more than one printed after his or her demise. For example, many prints by the German artist, Kaethe Kollwitz (1867-1945), exist in posthumous impressions and are so identified with a small embossed stamp just below the image. A signed impression, printed during the artist's lifetime, may sell for several thousand dollars and a posthumous restrike may only be worth a few hundred. It is important to determine just what you are looking at if it is not clearly identified.

In many cases, multiple editions of an artist's work exist and each edition usually has specific characteristics to distinguish it from the rest. The paper may vary, the ink color may change, the descriptive caption at the bottom of the design may read differently and so on. Regarding the Spanish artist, Francisco Goya (1746-1828), for example, many of his plates went through as many as eight or more editions with subtle changes occurring from one printing to the next. It is important to know what edition you are looking at, since as a general rule the earlier the printing the more valuable the print. Fortunately, Goya's prints are well catalogued and researched and there are specific books which describe the various editions. The works of many other artists, however, are not as well documented or there is virtually nothing at all to refer to. If this is the case for a print you have, try to find someone who can at least point you in the right direction.

RARITY

How rare is rare? How does rarity and the size of the edition affect the value of a print? The answer is simply that there is no precise, all-encompassing way to answer this, so the issue must be dealt with on a case by case basis. If, for example, the choice is between buying a rare Whistler lithograph or a Thomas Hart Benton (1889-1975) lithograph known to be printed in an edition of 250, the best decision, all other factors considered equal, is to buy the Whistler now because the Benton will almost certainly turn up again at a later date. The Whistler may not.

Remember that a small edition print, that is, one printed in fewer than twenty impressions, is simply not going to turn up as often as one which was printed in an edition of 250 impressions. Old master prints were generally printed as they were needed without a known, pre-established edition; hence the availability of a specific work can only be judged by how often it appears for sale on the market. For example, an important early italian engraving which hasn't turned up at auction for twenty years is bound to do well at auction today simply because it hasn't been available for a long time.

There are always exceptions, so don't necessarily be swayed by rarity as an all-important factor affecting value. A certain print may be extremely rare but it also may be extremely minor and unattractive. Only a few impressions of some prints exist because the artist was not satisfied with the results of his labor. Sometimes, a certain print simply did not sell to the public, so the edition was never completely printed. Just because something is considered "rare" does not necessarily enhance its desirability. "Rarity" can be used as a marketing ploy along with the word "Important." Don't let their true meanings be distorted.

STATES

An artist will often make changes and alterations in the initial design of a print and any such variation represents a change of *state*. A change of state can entail a reduction of the plate, additional work added to the image (a few more trees, perhaps, or more lines in the sky), or in the case of published prints, for example, a number or numeral may be added in the top right or left corner. Early states tend to be rare, in general, and they usually represent an "unfinished" artistic conception. The final state, or published state, represents the "completed" artistic conception and this is the state which turns up for sale most of the time. This is simply because far more impressions of the final state usually exist.

In terms of the marketplace, early states can at times be more interesting, more desirable and more valuable than the final state or the published state of a particular graphic work. In fact, sometimes later states of a print are posthumous impressions reworked by another hand. This is the case with many Rembrandt etchings and other old master prints.

Regarding the 19th century French etcher, Charles Meryon (1821-1868), for example, his early states tend to be more valuable since the artist, himself, did the printing. These impressions tend to be very dramatic, richly inked and especially appealing to the eye. The later states of most of his prints were professionally printed and although they are generally quite good, they do not command the same prices as the earlier impressions. This is a subtle matter, to be sure, but try to find out about the various states which comprise the development of a particular work of graphic art. There may be, for example, two states, four states, ten states or only one state.

A *catalogue raisonne*, a catalogue describing each print in detail, is available for most well-known artists and consulting such a publication will help you determine the state of a print (as well as providing other useful information). Knowing the state can assist you in assessing the value. This is just one more relevant factor which plays a part in determining the overall value of any given print.

Caution - Reproductive Prints

There are more reproductions available today than original prints. Most reproductions only qualify as decorative printed pictures. At one extreme we have the magnificent original prints by such artists as Durer, Rembrandt, Whistler and Jasper Johns; at the other end of the spectrum we have tedious reproductive steel engravings of old master paintings, colorful offset lithographs after Renoir's oil paintings and deceptive, confusing photogravure reproductions. The array is endless and the vast numbers of all kinds of prints in existence are enough to baffle the most serious student of fine original prints.

As a general rule, the more famous the artist the more susceptible the work is to being reproduced and copied. The French painter, Edouard Manet (1832-1883), produced many fine and desirable etchings after his own paintings but there are also innumerable photographic replicas of his paintings in existence which were printed by commercial companies. These are of no merit, whatsoever, even though they might well qualify as pretty, decorative pictures. In fact, with the invention of photography in the mid-nineteenth century, the world of printmaking was forever dramatically altered by new and innovative ways to reproduce the works of famous masters. The technology continues to evolve today as better and better reproductive prints are produced with slicker and slicker advertising packages to back them up - there is no end in sight.

Types of Reproductive Prints

There are basically three different types of reproductive prints to be aware of - reproductive engravings, photogravure reproductions and commercial offset lithographs. It is often difficult to differentiate these *reproductions* from *original* prints, due to the skill with which they were printed years ago, and due to the more recent innovations in photomechanical technology. *Caveat emptor - let the buyer beware!*

REPRODUCTIVE ENGRAVINGS

Before the camera was invented, popular paintings were copied by skilled craftsmen who worked primarily in engraving, etching and mezzotint. There is a seemingly endless supply of these works in existence and they tend to be highly detailed, elaborate, uncolored replicas done after oil paintings, watercolors and drawings. There are always exceptions to the rule but, for the most part, the frames are usually worth more today than the prints they showcase.

The typical reproductive engraving has printed information at the bottom which usually includes the painter's name and the engraver's name. The place of publication might also appear along with the title of the piece. For example, at the bottom left it might say "Jan Vermeer, pinxit" (pinxit means painted or painter) and at the bottom right some obscure engraver's name will usually appear with the word "sculpsit" or "fecit" (meaning etched by, engraved by or made by). Keep in mind there are several variants in the spelling of these terms and sometimes they aren't even used. There are *always* exceptions to the rules!

Although most reproductive engravings have decorative value only, often $100 or less, there are *many* prints done after paintings and watercolors which are indeed valuable. In fact, they can be very valuable especially when we consider the better English sporting prints, certain color floral prints and the engraved prints after John James Audubon, among others. (In keeping with the focus of this *Guide*, fine quality *decorative* prints will not be covered.)

The point here is that many reproductive engravings, especially those which bear the name of a well-known artist, can deceive the untrained viewer into thinking they are highly valuable. Just because the name Rembrandt, or Gainsborough, or Homer appears somewhere on the work, it does not necessarily mean this artist had anything to do with the making of the print itself. These reproductive engravings are, in effect, original reproductions.

PHOTOGRAVURE REPRODUCTIONS

Photogravures are among the most deceptive photomechanical reproductions ever made. Perfected during the second half of the nineteenth century, the photogravure process has produced some of the finest facsimiles of works by Durer, Rembrandt, Meryon and other well-known and important printmakers. Fortunately, many of the best photogravure reproductions are stamped on the verso identifying them as facsimile reproductions. Some, however, are not marked in any way and when framed and under glass, or just mounted, they can fool even the most seasoned print enthusiast. One of the best known firms, Amand-Durand, active in France in the 1870's and 1880's, made reproductions which are identified on the verso with the following small red ink stamp:

(twice actual size)

If you see this mark on the back of a print, you are looking at an inexpensive reproduction. They make important study pieces but they have little value.

The best way to appreciate and learn about photogravure reproductions is to place one next to an original of the same print. The line quality is different and the photogravure lacks the subtlety, the richness and the overall "character" of the original etching. Sometimes the platemark of a photogravure is not where it should be so be prepared to measure the overall dimensions to see if there is any appreciable difference. A *catalogue raisonne* will provide dimensions of the original print in question and if your measurements are off by up to one half inch, something is probably wrong. If you are not sure what you have, you should also consult a reliable dealer, an auction house, or a print curator at a local museum.

COMMERCIAL OFFSET LITHOGRAPHS

This modern day process has been a boon for large-scale, quantity-minded printing companies, but it has caused considerable problems for the world of fine prints. With this new technology, it became easy to print, *en masse*, colorful, deceptive reproductions of paintings, drawings and watercolors by old and modern masters.

This is especially the case for well-known 20th century European artists: Picasso, Dufy, Chagall, Miro, Dali, Buffet, Matisse and others. Their work has been subjected to innumerable commercial abuses of one kind or another and it is up to you to be an informed buyer. Consult a *catalogue raisonne* and other published information on the artist and print in question. Check with a reliable dealer and get an informed opinion (even if it means paying for an appraisal); consult with a museum curator about a work if you are in a position to do so; but always question what you are looking at and assume something is wrong with a piece until proven otherwise. This is especially advisable at small country auctions, for example, where the person who catalogued the prints is also responsible for oriental rugs, porcelains, paintings and any number of other collectibles. No one is an expert in all fields and mistakes are often made even when the most honorable intentions are involved!

For a detailed, thorough examination of reproductions, fakes and forgeries in the print world you should consult Theodore B. Donson's 1977 book, *Prints and the Print Market*. Further information about this and other publications relevant to our discussion is contained in the *Appendix*.

Pricing Your Print: A Summary

One thing for certain is that pricing and evaluating fine prints is not an exact science. This *Guide* will not necessarily provide a "quick fix" for every print which comes your way but we consider it an excellent place to start. If you know the name of the artist and the technique employed to produce the work (i.e., etching, engraving, lithograph, woodcut, etc.) you can refer to this *Guide* to determine a *potential* value for your print - assuming his/her name appears in the *Guide* to begin with.

The pursuit of a more precise fair market value can take much more time and energy than you want to expend. The print you have may be a rare state of a rare work by an important artist whose prints, unfortunately, seldom appear for sale - anywhere. The quickest and most reliable approach for pricing your print may be to have your print appraised, either verbally or in writing, by a print expert (i.e., print dealer, art dealer, or a print specialist at an auction house) - only they will have the accumulated knowledge, experience, and necessary references on hand to accurately assess your print's worth.

If you are determined to research the worth of your print yourself, you may want to consider the following multi-step process:

- Determine who authored the work and the technique employed (i.e., intaglio, relief, planographic).

- Knowing who the artist is and the printing technique employed, next check within this *Guide* to get an idea of the *potential* value for your print.

- Research the title of your piece by checking a *catalogue raisonne*, if available, for your artist. You will have to painstakingly take the time to match up your print with one in the *catalogue raisonne*. If you know that more than one *state* exists for your title, determine which *state* you have.

- Knowing who the artist was, the technique employed in producing the work, and the title of the print, you would now want to find previous sales of similarly titled prints to note what prices they had realized. The best place to check previous auction results is the many annuals now available to the collector and dealer. You may have to go back through several annuals to locate, hopefully with success, a previous sale of your similarly titled print. These important, and expensive references may be available at larger museums and public libraries. If you wish to begin purchasing these annuals for your personal library, you may find many art book dealers with these titles in stock. A list of titles can be found in the Appendix in the rear of this book.

- After you have noted the prices realized for prints of similar title to yours, keep in mind the additional effect of condition problems (i.e., foxing, stains, holes, tears, abrasions, etc.), if any, on the value of your print.

- And finally, *always remember that a reputable dealer is an invaluable resource, whose advice you should seek out as much as possible.*

CHAPTER TWO

Using This Guide

An Overview

The following information is provided by the publisher. Please read it thoroughly, so you will understand how the price entries in this *Guide* were derived. Remember, as explained in the previous chapter, we are focusing on fine art prints - including some important posters - and not the decorative prints (e.g., Currier & Ives, Audubon prints, city bird's eye views, etc.).

In the process of compiling the over 2,600 names of artists for this *Guide*, it was found that in many instances the spelling of names was incorrect or incomplete, with only initials and a surname, as they appeared in many of the auction house catalogs, nationally. This was due in part, understandably, to the haste with which many of these artists were researched and then recorded in the catalog in time for the pre-sale promotion. We recorded the full and correct spelling of names as accurately as possible by checking more than one dictionary of artists for each name. If no birth and death dates were available, the century during which that artist is known to have worked was placed next to the name. Also added, when available, was the nationality of the artist. If you are aware of any errors or omissions we would certainly like to hear from you. You are welcome and encouraged to comment, and feel free to suggest changes or additions which will improve this *Guide*.

Establishing Price Ranges

After carefully recording the auction prices for each artist for the last six years, we established a price range which reflected the "practical" low and high for that particular artist. If only one auction result could be found for an artist during the past six years, and it was deemed significant enough to report, we included it in this *Guide*. For consistency, we frequently rounded off odd prices to the next highest whole amount. In instances where very few auction results were available for a particular artist, we occasionally used the low end of a catalog estimate, if the print were passed, in establishing our price range for that artist.

Please keep in mind that, when looking at auction results, those prints which have previously sold may not have been the best or worst efforts by the artist. For this reason, in future auction sales, prints by artists listed herein may sell for far less or far more than previously. And never forget how **CONDITION** affects the value of a print!

Our Sources

In compiling the artists and prices for this *Guide* our most frequently used source was *Martin Gordon's Print Price Annual* - thru the 1993 edition. Most of the prices and/or price ranges entered in our *Guide* were compiled from the results reported in *Martin Gordon's Print Price Annual* for the past eight years (1986 to 1993). We found "Gordon's" to be, without question, the most comprehensive source for auction print price results, worldwide.

The published catalogs of prices paid for prints sold at auction during the 1992-1993 season provided another valuable source of price information. We researched print sales (through May, 1993) of the following leading auction houses and adjusted our prices accordingly. The addresses of these auction houses can be found in the *Appendix*.

- James R. Bakker Antiques, Inc., Massachusetts
- Butterfield & Butterfield, California
- Christie, Manson & Woods, London

- Christie, Manson & Woods, New York
- William Doyle Galleries, New York
- Leslie Hindman Auctions, Illinois
- Phillips, Son & Neale, London
- Robert W. Skinner, Massachusetts
- Sotheby's, London
- Sotheby's, New York
- Swann Galleries, New York
- Winter Associates, Connecticut

The Three Printing Techniques

In the previous chapter author William Carl discussed the three basic printing techniques available to an artist: intaglio, planographic, and relief. Some artists may have worked in only one technique throughout their career, but others may have worked in all three techniques.

When artists worked in more than one technique we found the prices realized at auction for each technique could be, in many instances, quite different. For example, an artist may have realized only a few hundred dollars for his etchings (intaglio technique) at auction, but realized several thousand dollars for his lithographs (planographic technique) at auction. Because each technique an artist employed could result in a different price range, we decided to research the prices realized for each technique and record them separately for your use. With many artists, you may find as many as three price ranges - one for each printing technique. On the other hand, many of the artists listed herein only worked in one technique and, therefore, will only have one entry.

In the alphabetical list of artists with prices, you will find the intaglio technique represented by "I", the planographic technique by "P", and the relief technique by "R". The following examples illustrates the format for presenting price ranges corresponding to the various techniques:

ACKERMANN, MAX (B.1887) GERMAN
  I/ 150-1300   P/ 75-1100
AMIET, CUNO (1868-1961) SWISS
  I/ 350-1200   P/ 75-2800   R/ 700-1100

Under each printing technique you may encounter the following types of prints (or combination of processes):

- **I** Intaglio
  o etching
  o drypoint
  o steel engraving
  o stipple engraving
  o aquatint
  o mezzotint
  o soft-ground etching
  o crayon manner

- **P** Planographic
  o lithograph
  o monotype
  o silk-screen
  o cliche verre
  o serigraph

- **R** Relief
  o wood block
    • woodcut
      o chiaroscuro
    • wood engraving
  o linoleum cut (linocut)

Artists in Dealer Catalogs

Beginning on page 199 William Carl has compiled an important alphabetical list of over 425 artists that rarely turn up at auctions but appear with frequency in numerous dealer catalogs across the country. The list emphasizes American, English, and French artists who produced prints primarily from 1860 to 1960. The price range given indicates where roughly 75% of an artist's works fall, price wise, based on a broad survey of numerous dealer catalogues. The printing technique listed is the technique for which he/she is best known. An asterisk after the ranges indicates that prints by this artist are *rare*.

"Le Couple" from LETTERA AMOROSA, 1963
by Georges Braque, lithograph
(Courtesy of Skinner, Inc., Bolton, MA)

DISCLAIMER

Although every attempt, within reason, has been made to keep the price ranges herein as accurate as possible, there may be mistakes, both typographical and in content. Therefore, this guide should be used only as a general guide not as the final or ultimate source of the only prices which may be realized at auction for prints by any particular artist. Remember, prints in very poor condition may realize only a fraction of the price realized for a similar print in excellent condition.

Special care must be exercised when examining the prices of prints by contemporary artists. With living artists, it is best to check with those galleries that represent them for the "final" word on current print prices. Prices charged in the galleries for the prints of living artists can often be many times those realized at auction.

Also, the compilation of auction houses and private dealers in the *Appendix* is only a representative sampling of the hundreds of auction houses and private dealers which may be of equal distinction.

The author and Currier Publications shall have neither liability nor responsibility to any person with respect to any loss or damage caused or alleged to be caused directly or indirectly by the information contained in this book.

Fine Art Prints
at Auction

ABBE, WILLIAM (20TH C) AMERICAN
I/ 40-100   R/ 30-100
ABELMAN, IDA (B. 1910) AMERICAN
P/ 40-300
ABLETT, WILLIAM (1877-1937) BRITISH
I/ 150-600   P/ 125
ABRAHAMS, IVOR (B. 1935) BRITISH
I/ 300   P/ 65-750
ABRAMS, WILLIAM R. (B. 1920) AMERICAN
R/ 25-100
ACHENBACH, ANDREAS (1815-1910) GERMAN
I/ 240   P/ 300
ACKERMANN, MAX (B. 1887) GERMAN
I/ 150-1100   P/ 75-1300
ACKERMANN, PETER (B. 1934) GERMAN
I/ 20-370
ADAM, ALBRECHT (1786-1862) GERMAN
I/ 170
ADAM, HENRI GEORGES (1904-1967) FRENCH
I/ 160
ADAMI, VALERIO (B. 1935) ITALIAN
I/ 100-450   P/ 25-621
ADAMS, KENNETH M. (1897-1966) AMERICAN
P/ 50-330
ADAMS, MARK (B. 1925) AMERICAN
I/ 300-700   P/ 330-950
ADDERLY, CHARLES (20TH C) AMERICAN
R/ 50-150
ADLER, JANKEL (1895-1949) POLISH
I/ 200-2500
AFFLECK, ANDREW F. (active 1910-1930) BRITISH
I/ 30-100
AFRO, BASADELLA (B. 1912) ITALIAN
I/ 360-11400   P/ 175-1900
AGAM, YAACOV (B. 1928) ISRAELI
P/ 50-2750

AGHIB, JOAN (20TH C) AMERICAN ?
I/ 50-150
AGOSTINI, TOBY (B. 1916) AMERICAN
P/ 500
AHLERS-HESTERMANN, FRITZ (B. 1883) GERMAN
P/ 60-250
AID, GEORGE C. (1872-1938) AMERICAN
I/ 25-100
AIKMAN, WALTER (1857-1939) AMERICAN
I/ 25-100
AIZPIRI, PAUL (B. 1919) FRENCH
P/ 150-2400
AKEN, JAN VAN (1614-1661) DUTCH
I/ 100-1000
AKERSLOOT, WILLEM (B. 1600) DUTCH
I/ 15000
ALBEE, GRACE (1890-1985) AMERICAN
R/ 35-1000
ALBERS, ANNI (B. 1899) AMERICAN
I/ 150-450   P/ 400
ALBERS, JOSEF (1888-1976) AMERICAN
I/ 600-900   P/ 10-4400   R/ 100-5280
ALBERT, HERMANN (B. 1937)
I/ 100-350
ALBERT-LASARD, L. (1891-1969) GERMAN
P/ 25-300
ALBERTI, CHERUBINO (1553-1615) ITALIAN
I/ 100-1500
ALBERTI, PIETRO FRANCESCO (1584-1638) ITALIAN
I/ 100-1000
ALBIKER, KARL (1878-1961) GERMAN
P/ 150-800
ALBRIGHT, IVAN LE LORRAINE (1897-1983) AMERICAN
P/ 350-5600
ALDEGREVER, HEINRICH (1502-1558) GERMAN
I/ 22-23100
ALDIN, CECIL CHARLES WINDSOR (1870-1935) BRITISH
I/ 175-1200   P/ 300
ALECHINSKY, PIERRE (B.1927) BELGIAN
I/ 25-34300   P/ 25-1100   R/ 25-1512
ALESI, HUGO DE (1840-1906) FRENCH
P/ 40-850
ALEXEIEFF, ALEX (1901-1982) RUSSIAN
I/ 25   P/ 4000-21000

ALLEN, JAMES E. (1894-1964) AMERICAN
  I/ 300-7150   P/ 40-800
ALMELOVEEN, JAN VAN (17TH C) DUTCH
  I/ 100-250   P/ 2750
ALOISI, GIOVANNI (active Ca. 1600) ITALIAN
  I/ 7000
ALT, OTMAR (B. 1940) GERMAN
  I/ 145-275   P/ 25-1100   R/ 30-150
ALTDORFER, ALBRECHT (1480-1538) GERMAN
  I/ 150-25000   R/ 120-40000
ALTENBOURG, GERHARD (20TH C) GERMAN
  I/ 300-480   R/ 100-4100   P/ 100-1400
ALTHIEM, WILHELM (1871-1914) GERMAN
  I/ 200-500
ALTMAN, HAROLD (B. 1925) AMERICAN
  I/ 50-850   R/ 2700   P/ 100-1500
AMAN-JEAN, EDMOND FRANCOIS (1860-1935) FRENCH
  I/ 250   P/ 275-1500
AMATO, FRANCESCO (17TH C) ITALIAN
  I/ 600
AMELIN, ALBIN (B. 1902) SWEDISH ?
  P/ 150-1500
AMEN, IRVING (B. 1918) AMERICAN
  P/ 75-200   R/ 30-100
AMENOFF, GREGORY (B. 1948) AMERICAN
  R/ 1100-1925   P/ 220
AMERO, EMILIO (20TH C) MEXICAN
  P/ 50-400
AMIET, CUNO (1868-1961) SWISS
  I/ 350-1200   P/ 75-2820   R/ 700-1100
AMIGONI, JACOPO (1682-1752) ITALIAN
  I/ 200-950
AMLING, KARL GUSTAV (1651-1702) GERMAN
  I/ 350
AMMAN, JOST (1539-1591) GERMAN
  I/ 10-4500   R/ 25-300
AMTSBERG, OTTO (19TH/20TH C) NORWEGIAN
  P/ 600-2000
ANDERSON, C.W. (20TH C) AMERICAN
  P/ 50-25O
ANDERSON, STANLEY (1884-1966) BRITISH
  I/ 75-600
ANDREA, ZOAN (active 1475-1505) ITALIAN
  I/ 600-25000

ANDREANI, ANDREA (1560-1623) ITALIAN
 R/ 100-6300
ANDREENKO, MIKHAIL (1895-1982) RUSSIAN
 P/ 300-600
ANDREWS, SYBIL (B. 1898) BRITISH
 I/ 300-650   R/ 200-8400
ANDRI, FERDINAND (19TH/20TH C)
 P/ 100-428   R/ 120
ANTES, HORST (B.1936) GERMAN
 I/ 60-7800   P/ 25-1950
ANTHONY, CAROL (B. 1943) AMERICAN
 P/ 50-1100
ANUSKIEWICZ, RICHARD (B. 1930) AMERICAN
 P/ 44-660   R/ 20-300
APPEL, KAREL (B.1921) DUTCH/AMERICAN
 I/ 200-3800   P/ 25-7000   R/ 300-8500
APPIAN, JACQUES B. (Called ADOLPHE) (1818-1898) FRENCH
 I/ 75-700
ARAKAWA, SHUSAKU (B.1936) JAPANESE
 I/ 1200-1700   P/ 200-6050
ARCANGELO, ALLAN D' (B. 1930) AMERICAN
 P/ 110-880
ARCHIPENKO, ALEXANDER (1887-1964) RUSSIAN
 I/ 7000   P/ 75-7600
ARMAN, (ARMAN FERNANDEZ) (B. 1928) FRENCH
 I/ 297-2300   P/ 50-4800
ARMINGTON, FRANK M. (1876-1940) AMERICAN
 I/ 25-100
ARMS, JOHN TAYLOR (1887-1953) AMERICAN
 I/ 50-8800   P/ 187
ARNESON, ROBERT (20TH C) AMERICAN
 I/ 75-1100   P/ 350-1100   R/ 660
ARNHOLD, JOHANN (1766-1828) GERMAN
 P/ 1500-4600
ARNOLDI, CHARLES (B. 1946) AMERICAN
 I/ 90-1300   P/ 100-6100   R/ 70-400
ARP, JEAN (HANS) (1887-1966) FRENCH
 I/ 25-1500   P/ 100-3600   R/ 50-6000
ARPKE, OTTO (20TH C) ?
 P/ 800-3100
ARROYO, EDUARDO (B. 1937) SPANISH
 P/ 100-450
ARTSCHWAGER, RICHARD (B. 1924) AMERICAN
 I/ 3080   P/ 1000-4000

ARTZYBASHEFF, BORIS (1899-1965) RUSSIAN/AMERICAN
  R/ 300-750
ASMUS, DIETER (B. 1939) ?
  P/ 125-3600
ASSCH, FRANK H. (19TH/20TH C) AMERICAN
  P/ 900
ASSELIN, MAURICE (1882-1947) FRENCH
  P/ 197-275
ATCHE, JANE (19TH C) FRENCH
  P/ 900-3800
ATLAN, JEAN-MICHEL (1913-1960) FRENCH
  P/ 200-2700
ATTERSEE, CHRISTIAN (B. 1941) ?
  P/ 100-500
AUBERJONOIS, RENE (1872-1957) SWISS
  P/ 100-1200
AUERBACH, FRANK (B. 1931) AMERICAN
  I/ 11500   P/ 200-850
AUGER, ADRIEN V. (B. 1787) FRENCH
  P/ 300
AUSTIN, ROBERT S. (1895-1973) BRITISH
  I/ 100-850
AVATI, MARIO (B. 1921) FRENCH
  I/ 100-1400
AVERY, MILTON (1893-1965) AMERICAN
  I/ 160-6600   P/ 110-2090   R/ 300-4000
AVRIL, JEAN JACQUES (1744-1831) FRENCH
  I/ 1200
AXELROD, EILEEN (20TH C) AMERICAN
  I/ 25-150
AZOULAY, GUILLAUME A. (B. 1949) MOROCCO
  I/ 75-450

B

BABOULENE, EUGENE (B. 1905) FRENCH
  P/ 100-400
BAC, FERNAND (1859-1952) FRENCH
  P/ 400-3500
BACH, ELVIRA (20TH C) GERMAN

P/ 500-1800
BACHEM, BELE (B. 1916) GERMAN
P/ 25-500
BACHILOFF, M. (19TH C) RUSSIAN
I/ 20-80
BACHMANN, OTTO (19TH C) GERMAN
P/ 56-2430
BACKHUIZEN, LUDOLF (1631-1708) DUTCH
I/ 51-1256
BACON, FRANCIS (B. 1909) BRITISH
I/ 800-8100   P/ 25-31000
BACON, PEGGY B. (1895-1987) AMERICAN
I/ 150-2100   P/ 150-660
BADMIN, STANLEY ROY (B. 1906) BRITISH
I/ 200-750
BAECHLER, DONALD (B. 1956) AMERICAN
I/ 300-1200   P/ 2500-4500   R/ 3850
BAEDER, JOHN (B. 1938) AMERICAN
P/ 30-12000
BAERTLING, OLLE (1911-1981)
P/ 50-2500
BAIER, JEAN (B. 1932) SWISS
I/ 50-400
BAILEY, VERNON H. (1874-1953) AMERICAN
P/ 25-100
BAILEY, WILLIAM H. (B. 1930) AMERICAN
I/ 250-4950   P/ 700-2900
BAJ, ENRICO (B. 1924) ITALIAN
I/ 50-3100   P/ 60-1300
BALDUNG, HANS (1484-1545) GERMAN
R/ 139-46000
BALESTRIERI, LIONELLO (1872-1958) ITALIAN
I/ 300
BALLINGER, R. MAXIL (B. 1914) AMERICAN
R/ 25-100
BALTEN, PIETER (1525-1598) FLEMISH
I/ 200-300
BALUSCHEK, HANS (B. 1870) GERMAN
P/ 200-750
BARBARI, JACOPO DE (1440-1516) ITALIAN
I/ 300-19000
BARBATELLI, BERNARDO (1548-1612) ITALIAN
I/ 12000
BARBIER, GEORGES (1882-1932) FRENCH

Technique Key

Under each printing technique you may encounter the following types of prints (or combination of processes):

- **I** Intaglio:
  - etching
  - drypoint
  - steel engraving
  - stipple engraving
  - aquatint
  - mezzotint
  - soft-ground etching
  - crayon manner

- **P** Planographic:
  - lithograph
  - monotype
  - silk-screen
  - cliche verre
  - serigraph

- **R** Relief:
  - wood block
    - woodcut
      - chiaroscuro
    - wood engraving
  - linoleum cut (linocut)

P/ 1500-4620　　R/ 15000
BARBIERE, DOMENICO (1506-1565) ITALIAN
　I/ 100-9800
BARGHEER, EDUARD (B. 1901) GERMAN
　I/ 25-6000　　P/ 25-2500　　R/ 50-300
BARLACH, ERNST (1870-1938) GERMAN
　P/ 50-8820　　R/ 25-13100
BARNET, WILL (B. 1911) AMERICAN
　I/ 165-2800　　P/ 50-5400　　R/ 500-3100
BAROCCI, FEDERICO (1526-1612) ITALIAN
　I/ 300-9800　　R/ 500-4000
BARR, NORMAN (B. 1908) AMERICAN
　P/ 100-450
BARRAUD, MAURICE (1889-1955) SWISS
　I/ 25-1500　　P/ 100-900　　R/ 311
BARRERE, ADRIEN (1877-1931) FRENCH
　P/ 500-8800
BARRETT, HOPE B. (20TH C) AMERICAN
　R/ 25-100
BARRIBAL, W. H. (?) BRITISH
　P/ 2700
BARRY, JAMES (1741-1806) BRITISH
　I/ 1500-12000　　P/ 1600-7100
BARTLETT, ELWOOD (B. 1906) AMERICAN
　R/ 25-100
BARTLETT, JENNIFER (B. 1941) AMERICAN
　I/ 3500-7500　　P/ 440-55000　　R/ 900-7980
BARTLETT, CHARLES WILLIAM (1860-1940) BRITISH
　R/ 150-825
BARTOLOZZI, FRANCESCO (1727-1815) ITALIAN
　I/ 100-6200
BARTON, LOREN (1893-1975) AMERICAN
　I/ 25-100
BARTSCH, ADAM VON (1757-1821) AUSTRIAN
　I/ 75-2800
BASAN, PIERRE FRANCOIS (1723-1797) FRENCH
　I/ 150-300
BASELITZ, GEORG (B. 1938) GERMAN
　I/ 125-20000　　P/ 2250　　R/ 300-31000
BASKIN, LEONARD (B. 1922) AMERICAN
　I/ 40-2400　　P/ 100-1320　　R/ 30-1500
BASQUIAT, JEAN M. (20TH C) AMERICAN
　P/ 200-30250
BASSE, WILHELM (B. 1613) DUTCH

I/ 600
BASSET (18TH/19TH C) FRENCH
   I/ 400   P/ 600
BASTARD, MARC A. (B. 1863) SWISS
   P/ 850-1200
BATE, STANLEY (B. 1903) AMERICAN
   I/ 30-125
BATTKE, HEINZ (1900-1966) GERMAN
   I/ 100-175
BAUDOUIN, PIERRE ANTOINE (1723-1769) FRENCH
   I/ 300-400
BAUER, CARL (20TH C) FRENCH
   I/ 30-100   P/ 190
BAUER, MARIUS A. J. (1867-1932) DUTCH
   I/ 100-200
BAUER, RUDOLF (1889-1953) GERMAN
   I/ 100-400   P/ 125-1900
BAUKNECHT, PHILIPP (1884-1933) GERMAN
   I/ 300   R/ 150-1900
BAUM, CARL (CHARLES ?) (19TH C) AMERICAN
   I/ 150
BAUM, PAUL (1859-1932) GERMAN
   I/ 150-550   P/ 400-800
BAUMANN, GUSTAVE (1881-1971) AMERICAN
   P/ 800   R/ 200-5500
BAUMBACH, HAROLD (20TH C) AMERICAN
   P/ 25-100
BAUMBERGER, OTTO (20TH C) GERMAN
   P/ 200-4000
BAUMEISTER, WILLI (1889-1955) GERMAN
   I/ 2400   P/ 50-16000   R/ 1000-1500
BAXTER, GEORGE (1804-1867) BRITISH
   I/ 700
BAY, H. (20TH C) EUROPEAN
   I/ 10-50
BAYER, HERBERT (B. 1900) AMERICAN
   P/ 75-17600
BAYLAC, LUCIEN (19TH C) FRENCH
   P/ 350-1320
BAYNARD, ED (B. 1940) AMERICAN
   I/ 200-2200   R/ 400-2700
BAYROS, FRANZ VON (1866-1924) GERMAN
   I/ 50-2000
BAZAINE, JEAN RENE (B. 1904) FRENCH

I/ 100-550   P/ 100-500
BAZICALUVA, ERCOLE (17TH C) ITALIAN
     I/ 100-500
BEAL, JACK (B. 1931) AMERICAN
     P/ 25-350   R/ 385
BEAL, REYNOLDS (1867-1951) AMERICAN
     I/ 50-4130
BEARDEN, ROMARE (1914-1988) AMERICAN
     I/ 1043-3500   P/ 275-4500
BEARDSLEY, AUBREY (1872-1898) BRITISH
     P/ 100-5500
BEATRIZET, NICOLAS (1515-1565) FRENCH
     I/ 40-4900
BEAUDIN, ANDRE (1895-1980) FRENCH
     I/ 186   P/ 20-1100
BEAUFRERE, ADOLPH-MARIE-TIMOTHEE (1876-1960) FRENCH
     I/ 25-700   R/ 4700
BEAUSSIER, EMILE (B. 1874) FRENCH
     P/ 800
BEAUVARLET, JACQUES-FIRMIN (1731-1797) FRENCH
     I/ 200-525
BECCAFUMI, DOMENICO (1486-1551) ITALIAN
     I/ 8500-90000   R/ 36000
BECHTLE, ROBERT ALAN (B. 1932) AMERICAN
     I/ 800-1600   P/ 300-600
BECK, LEONHARD (1480-1542) GERMAN
     R/ 25-11000
BECKMANN, MAX (1884-1950) GERMAN/AMERICAN
     I/ 45-173000   P/ 25-78000   R/ 185-40000
BEERI, TUVIA (B. 1929) ISRAELI
     I/ 75-275
BEGA, CORNELIS PIETERSZ (1620-1664) DUTCH
     I/ 22-4100
BEHAM, BARTHEL (1502-1540) GERMAN
     I/ 100-37800   R/ 350
BEHAM, HANS SEBALD (1500-1550) GERMAN
     I/ 25-32000   R/ 25-4600
BEHMER, MARCUS (1879-1958) GERMAN
     I/ 25-700   R/ 250-1600
BEHRENS, PETER (1868-1940) GERMAN
     P/ 500-8000   R/ 175-4900
BEJOT, EUGENE (1867-1931) FRENCH
     I/ 75-600
BELL, LARRY (B. 1939) AMERICAN

P/ 500-1300
BELLA, STEFANO DELLA (1610-1664) ITALIAN
I/ 40-7300
BELLANGE, JACQUES (1594-1638) FRENCH
I/ 75-87300
BELLANGE, JOSEPH L.H. (1800-1866) FRENCH
P/ 25-75
BELLING, RUDOLF (B. 1886) GERMAN
P/ 90-340
BELLMER, HANS (1902-1975) FRENCH
I/ 25-7400   P/ 100-1300
BELLONI, GIORGIO (1861-1944)
P/ 300-2640 (monotypes only)
BELLOTTO, BERNARDO (1724-1780) ITALIAN
I/ 800-20000
BELLOWS, ALBERT F. (1829-1883) AMERICAN
I/ 25-100
BELLOWS, GEORGE W. (1882-1925) AMERICAN
P/ 250-86000
BELON, JOSE (D. 1927) FRENCH
P/ 425
BEMMEL, PETER VON (1685-1754) GERMAN
I/ 50-300
BENAZECH, CHARLES (1767-1794) BRITISH
I/ 503-1100
BENDINER, ALFRED (B. 1899) AMERICAN
P/ 25-100
BENGSTON, BILLY AL (B. 1934) AMERICAN
P/ 150-700
BENNETT, ALFRED J. (B. 1891) AMERICAN
I/ 20-100
BENNETT, WILLIAM JAMES (1787-1844) AMERICAN
I/ 500-20900
BENSON, FRANK WESTON (1862-1951) AMERICAN
I/ 200-2000   P/ 473-500
BENTON, THOMAS HART (1889-1975) AMERICAN
P/ 275-23100
BERCHEM, NICOLAES (1620-1683) DUTCH
I/ 130-6200
BERCHMANS, EMILE (B. 1867) BELGIAN
P/ 50-880
BERGERE, RICHARD (B. 1912) AMERICAN
P/ 25-100
BERGES, WERNER (B. 1941) GERMAN

P/ 80-325
BERGMEISTER, HERMANN (B. 1869) GERMAN
I/ 20-100
BERKE, HUBERT (B. 1908) GERMAN
R/ 25-350
BERNARD, DAVID (B. 1913) AMERICAN
I/ 25-100
BERNARD, EMILE (1868-1941) FRENCH
I/ 50-500   P/ 1400-10000   R/ 200-18000
BERNASCONI, F. (19TH C) ITALIAN
P/ 1500
BERNDT, SIEGFRIED (B. 1880) GERMAN
R/ 100-175
BERRY, CARROLL THAYER (1886-1978) AMERICAN
R/ 50-400
BERTANI, GIOVANNI-BATTISTA (1516-1576) ITALIAN
I/ 250
BERTHON, PAUL (1872-1909) FRENCH
P/ 40-2640
BERTOIA, HARRY (1915-1978) AMERICAN
P/ 1000-3000
BERTON, ARMAND (B. 1854-1927) FRENCH
I/ 100-300   P/ 50-350
BESNARD, PAUL ALBERT (1849-1934) FRENCH
I/ 50-2200   P/ 100-650
BETHERS, RAY (B. 1902) AMERICAN
R/ 25-100
BEURDELEY, JACQUES (1874-1954) FRENCH
I/ 40-260
BEUYS, JOSEF (1921-1986) GERMAN
I/ 400-5000   P/ 35-16500   R/ 1955-15000
BEVAN, ROBERT (1865-1925) BRITISH
P/ 400-2800
BEVERLOO, CORNELIS VAN (B. 1922) FRENCH
P/ 75-450
BEWICK, THOMAS (1753-1828) BRITISH
R/ 150-600
BICKEL, KARL (20TH C)
P/ 300-4800
BICKNELL, WILLIAM HENRY WARREN (1860-1947) AMERICAN
I/ 60-220
BIDDLE, GEORGE (1885-1973) AMERICAN
P/ 30-375
BIGOT, GEORGES (19TH C) FRENCH

I/ 3000
BILL, MAX (B. 1908) SWISS
   I/ 310   P/ 25-8000   R/ 400-1300
BILLINGS, HENRY (B. 1901) AMERICAN
   P/ 75-150
BILLMYER, JOHN (B. 1912) AMERICAN
   I/ 30-100
BINCK, JACOB (1500-1569) GERMAN
   I/ 97-6500
BINDER, JOSEPH (1805-1863) AUSTRIAN
   P/ 400-900
BIRCH, WILLIAM (1755-1834) AMERICAN
   I/ 400-1600
BISCAINO, BARTOLOMMEO (1632-1657) ITALIAN
   I/ 75-5100
BISCHOFF, HENRY (1882-1951) SWISS
   R/ 80-150
BISHOP, ISABEL (1902-1988) AMERICAN
   I/ 150-2750
BISHOP, RICHARD EVETT (1887-1975) AMERICAN
   I/ 50-1100
BISSCHOP, JAN DE (1628-1671) DUTCH
   I/ 175-700
BISSIER, JULES (1893-1965) GERMAN/SWISS
   P/ 100-5900   R/ 600-1400
BISSIERE, ROGER (1884-1964) FRENCH
   I/ 150-500   P/ 100-900   R/ 1445
BISTTRAM, EMIL (1895-1976) AMERICAN
   P 500
BLAKE, PETER (B. 1932) BRITISH
   I/ 510   P/ 40-600
BLAKE, WILLIAM (1757-1827) BRITISH
   I/ 50-92500   P/ 41000
BLAMPIED, EDMUND (1886-1966) BRITISH
   I/ 25-2000   P/ 350-750   R/ 200
BLAUSTEIN, AL (B. 1924) AMERICAN
   I/ 20-75
BLECHEN, KARL (1798-1840) GERMAN
   I/ 500-600   P/ 1400-5300
BLECKNER, ROSS (B. 1949) AMERICAN
   P/ 750-3900
BLEKER, GERRIT C. (active 1625-1656) DUTCH
   I/ 150-3200
BLEYL, FRITZ (B. 1881) GERMAN

Technique Key

Under each <u>printing technique</u> you may encounter the following types of prints (or combination of processes):

- **I** <u>Intaglio:</u>
  - etching
  - drypoint
  - steel engraving
  - stipple engraving
  - aquatint
  - mezzotint
  - soft-ground etching
  - crayon manner

- **P** <u>Planographic:</u>
  - lithograph
  - monotype
  - silk-screen
  - cliche verre
  - serigraph

- **R** <u>Relief:</u>
  - wood block
    - woodcut
      - chiaroscuro
    - wood engraving
  - linoleum cut (linocut)

R/ 250-3000
BLOCH, LUCIENNE (B. 1909) AMERICAN
   P/ 150
BLOEMAERT, ABRAHAM (1564-1651) DUTCH
   I/ 50-1100   R/ 350-3000
BLOMAERT, CORNELIS (1603-1680) DUTCH
   I/ 300-400
BLOOTELING, ABRAHAM (1640-1690) BRITISH
   I/ 50-450
BLOTT, GEORGE (19TH/20TH C) FRENCH
   P/ 250-1400
BOBLETER, LOWELL (1902-1973) AMERICAN
   I/ 25-100
BOCHNER, MEL (B. 1940) AMERICAN
   I/ 200-2200
BOCKSTIEGEL, PETER (1889-1951) GERMAN
   I/ 200-1900   P/ 750-4800   R/ 1120
BODMER, KARL (1809-1893) SWISS
   P/ 250-9400
BOEHLE, FRITZ (1873-1916) GERMAN
   I/ 75-1300
BOEL, PETER (1622-1674) FRENCH
   I/ 350
BOHL, WALTER (20TH C) AMERICAN
   I/ 15-50
BOHROD, AARON (1907-1992) AMERICAN
   P/ 25-250
BOISSIEU, JEAN-JACQUES DE (1736-1810) FRENCH
   I/ 50-1150
BOL, FERDINAND (1616-1680) DUTCH
   I/ 50-31000
BOLDRINI, NICOLO (B. 1510) ITALIAN
   I/ 350   R/ 100-1100
BOLSWERT, BOETIUS (1580-1633) DUTCH
   I/ 200-800
BOLSWERT, SCHELTE (1586-1659) DUTCH
   I/ 150-1600
BOLTON, CLARENCE (1893 1962) AMERICAN
   P/ 25-100
BOMBLED, LOUIS CHARLES (1862-1927) FRENCH
   P/ 300-800
BOMBERG, DAVID (1890-1957) BRITISH
   P/ 400-750
BONACINO, G. (19TH C) ITALIAN

I/ 750
BONASONE, GIULIO (1498-1580) ITALIAN
   I/ 25-6000
BONE, SIR MUIRHEAD (1876-1953) SCOTTISH
   I/ 100-4700   P/ 50-575
BONI, PAOLO (B. 1926) ITALIAN
   I/ 100-575
BONINGTON, RICHARD PARKES (1802-1828) BRITISH
   I/ 50-300   P/ 50-1300
BONNANO, CARMEN (20TH C) AMERICAN
   I/ 50-125
BONNARD, PIERRE (1867-1947) FRENCH
   I/ 50-2200   P/ 75-268000
BONNET, LOUIS MARIN (1736-1793) FRENCH
   I/ 125-82000
BONTECOU, LEE (B. 1931) AMERICAN
   P/ 50-850
BORCHT, HENDRIK VAN DER II (B. 1614) DUTCH
   I/ 800
BOREIN, EDWARD (1873-1945) AMERICAN
   I/ 200-2500
BORG, CARL OSCAR (1879-1947) AMERICAN
   I/ 400-950   R/ 300-1000
BORGIANI, H. (16TH C) ITALIAN
   I/ 200
BORGIANNI, ORAZIO (1578-1616) ITALIAN
   I/ 25-4800
BOROFSKY, JONATHAN (B. 1942) AMERICAN
   I/ 11000   P/ 400-13200
BORTNYIK, SANDOR (B. 1893) HUNGARIAN
   P 200-600
BOS, B.VAN DEN (1518-1580) FLEMISH
   I/ 100-850
BOS, CORNELIS (1506-1570) FRENCH
   I/ 100-1600
BOSCOVITZ, FRITZ (B. 1871) SWISS
   P/ 100-1600
BOSMAN, RICHARD (B. 1944) AMERICAN
   I/ 350-880   R/ 220-3575
BOSSE, ABRAHAM (1602-1676) FRENCH
   I/ 125-5700
BOTERO, FERNANDO (B. 1932) COLOMBIAN
   P/ 1000-6050
BOTH, JAN (1618-1652) DUTCH

I/ 75-3500
BOTT, FRANCIS (B. 1904) GERMAN
   I/ 250-600   P/ 40-1600
BOTTGER, KALUS (1942) GERMAN
   I/ 75-550
BOTTINI, GEORGES (1874-1907) FRENCH
   I/ 1300-2400   P/ 1500-7200   R/ 900
BOTTS, HUGH (1903-1964) AMERICAN
   I/ 20-75
BOUDIN, EUGENE (1824-1898) FRENCH
   I/ 150-1100   P/ 350
BOUISSET, FIRMIN (1859-1925) FRENCH
   P/ 600-4000
BOULANGER, GUSTAVE C. (1824-1888) FRENCH
   P/ 450-500
BOULLOGNE, LOUIS DE II (1654-1733) FRENCH
   I/ 250
BOURDON, SEBASTIEN (1616-1671) FRENCH
   I/ 150-300
BOURGEOIS DU CASTELET, FLORENT F. C. (1767-1836) FRENCH
   P/ 100
BOUT, PEETER (1658-1719) FLEMISH
   I/ 450-6600
BOUTET, HENRI (1851-1919) FRENCH
   I/ 30-275   P/ 15-1500
BOYD, FISKE (1895-1975) AMERICAN
   I/ 30   R/ 100-300
BOYDELL, JOHN (1719-1804) BRITISH
   I/ 100
BOYER, RALPH L. (1879-1952) AMERICAN
   I/ 25-100
BRACQUEMOND, FELIX (1833-1914) FRENCH
   I/ 25-9900   R/ 350
BRADFORD, HOWARD (B. 1919) AMERICAN
   P/ 20-60
BRADLEY, WILLIAM H. (1868-1962) AMERICAN
   I/ 70-5500   P/ 800-5000
BRAEU, NICHOLAS DE (17TH C) DUTCH
   I/ 725
BRANGWYN, SIR FRANK (1867-1956) BRITISH
   I/ 25-1200   P/ 50-2000   R/ 25-600
BRAQUE, GEORGES (1882-1963) FRENCH
   I/ 175-93500   P/ 50-56000   R/ 275-15400
BRASILIER, ANDRE (B. 1929) FRENCH

I/ 2750   P/ 90-6200   R/ 1130
BRAUER, ARIK (B.1929) GERMAN
I/ 50-600   P/ 100-450
BRAUER, ERICH (B. 1929) AUSTRIAN
I/ 100-600   P/ 150
BRAUNER, VICTOR (1903-1966) RUMANIAN
I/ 375-1900   P/ 100-755
BRAYER, YVES (B. 1907) FRENCH
I/ 126-350   P/ 25-6000
BREAUTE, ALBERT (B. 1853) FRENCH
P/ 200
BREBIETTE, PIERRE (1598-1650) FRENCH
I/ 100-400
BRECKERVELD, HERMAN (17TH C) DUTCH
I/ 300
BREITER, HERBERT (B. 1923) GERMAN
P/ 20-325
BREMER, UWE (B. 1940) GERMAN
I/ 12-600   R/ 145-300
BRENDEL, KARL A. (B. 1877) GERMAN
R/ 150
BRENOT, PIERRE LAURENT (B. 1913) FRENCH
P/ 300
BRESCIA, GIOVANNI (16TH C) ITALIAN
I/ 900-62000
BRESDIN, RODOLPHE (1822-1885) FRENCH
I/ 77-16000   P/ 200-47000
BRESSLERN-ROTH, NORBERTINE (1891-1978) AUSTRIAN/AMERICAN
R/ 100-525
BREUIL, A. (?) FRENCH
P/ 700
BRIANCHON, MAURICE (B. 1899) FRENCH
P/ 100-400
BRIGHTWELL, LEONARD R. (active 1925-38) BRITISH
I/ 25-100
BRIGNONI, SERGE (B. 1903) ITALIAN
P/ 75-800
BRIOT, ISAAC II (1585-1670) FRENCH
I/ 1100
BRISCHLE, EMIL (B. 1884) GERMAN
P/ 250
BRISCOE, ARTHUR JOHN TREVOR (1873-1943) BRITISH
I/ 75-900
BRIZZIO, FRANCESCO (1574-1623) ITALIAN

I/ 150-750
BROCKHURST, GERALD LESLIE (1890-1978) BRITISH
I/ 100-15400   P/ 130-990   R/ 100-300
BROCKHUSEN, THEO (19TH/20TH C) GERMAN
I/ 200-425
BRODOVITCH, ALEXEV (1898-1971) AMERICAN
P/ 1800
BROODTHAERS, MARCEL (B. 1924) BELGIAN
P/ 500-8000
BROOKS, JAMES (20TH C) AMERICAN
P/ 30-100
BROOKS, MILDRED B. (B. 1901) AMERICAN
I/ 200
BROOKSHAW, GEORGE (?) BRITISH
I/ 150
BROSAMER, HANS (1506-1554) GERMAN
I/ 100-3500   R/ 768
BROUET, AUGUSTE (1872-1941) FRENCH
I/ 40-700
BROWN, BOLTON (COIT)(1865-1936) AMERICAN
P/ 50-125
BROWN, HAROLD HAVEN (1869-1932) AMERICAN
R/ 40-100
BRUN, EDME GUSTAVE FREDERIC (1817-1881) FRENCH
P/ 375 500
BRUNELLESCHI, UMBERTO (20TH C) ITALIAN
I/ 150-830   P/ 400-2600
BRUNI, BRUNO (FRANCESCO) (1648-1726)
I/ 120-275   P/ 75-610
BRUNING, PETER (1929-1970) GERMAN
I/ 1000-2100   P/ 70-1300
BRUS, GUNTER (B. 1938) AUSTRIAN
I/ 100-1200   P/ 100
BRUSTOLON, GIOVANNI (B. 1726) ITALIAN
I/ 200-2200
BRUYCKER, JULES DE (1870-1945) BELGIAN
I/ 400-800
BRUYN, NICHOLAS DE (17TH C) DUTCH
I/ 25-1700
BRY, JAN THEODOR DE (1528-1598) FLEMISH
I/ 100-3894
BUCHHEISTER, CARL (KARL) (1890-1964) GERMAN
I/ 10-1600   P/ 630-690
BUCHHOLZ, ERICH (B. 1891) GERMAN

P/ 50-1300   R/ 227
BUCHHOLZ, WOLFF (B. 1935) GERMAN
    I/ 50-500   P/ 75-250
BUCKLEY, STEPHEN (B. 1944) BRITISH
    P/ 600-1200
BUELL, ALICE STANDISH (B. 1892) AMERICAN
    I/ 50-200
BUFANO, REMO (B. 1894) AMERICAN
    P/ 300
BUFFET, BERNARD (B. 1928) FRENCH
    I/ 40-22000   P/ 40-39600
BUHOT, FELIX HILAIRE (1847-1898) FRENCH
    I/ 45-9200   P/ 100-2700
BUNBURY, HENRY W. (1750-1811) BRITISH
    I/ 800
BURCHARTZ, MAX (1887-1961) GERMAN
    P/ 150-8000
BURCHFIELD, CHARLES E. (1893-1967) AMERICAN
    I/ 4620   P/ 2600-9900
BURGKMAIR, HANS (1473-1531) GERMAN
    I/ 200-5500   R/ 100-164000
BURKNER, HUGO (19TH C) GERMAN
    I/ 400
BURLIUK, DAVID (1882-1966) AMERICAN
    P/ 392-1650
BURNS, MILTON J. (B. 1953) AMERICAN
    I/ 25-100
BURR, GEORGE ELBERT (1859-1939) AMERICAN
    I/ 125-1200
BURRA, EDWARD (1905-1976) BRITISH
    I/ 100-300   R/ 100
BURRELL, ALFRED R. (B. 1877) AMERICAN
    I/ 25-250
BURRI, ALBERTO (B. 1915) ITALIAN
    I/ 500-4600   P/ 2300
BUSINCK, LUDOLPH (B. 1635) GERMAN
    R/ 225-3700
BUSSE, GEORG (1810-1868) GERMAN
    I/ 150-600
BUSSENMACHER, JOHANN (active 1580-1613) GERMAN
    I/ 400
BUTHE, MICHAEL (B. 1944) AMERICAN
    I/ 200-1100   P/ 150-400
BUTLER, REG (B. 1913) BRITISH

Technique Key

Under each <u>printing technique</u> you may encounter the following types of prints (or combination of processes):

- **I** <u>Intaglio:</u>
  - etching
  - drypoint
  - steel engraving
  - stipple engraving
  - aquatint
  - mezzotint
  - soft-ground etching
  - crayon manner

- **P** <u>Planographic:</u>
  - lithograph
  - monotype
  - silk-screen
  - cliche verre
  - serigraph

- **R** <u>Relief:</u>
  - wood block
    - woodcut
      - chiaroscuro
    - wood engraving
  - linoleum cut (linocut)

P/ 150-550
BYE, MARCUS DE (1639-1688) DUTCH
I/ 50-150
BYXBE, LYMAN (1886-1966) AMERICAN
I/ 25-100

C

CADMUS, PAUL (B. 1904) AMERICAN
I/ 300-9350   P/ 200-1020
CADY, HARRISON (1877-1970) AMERICAN
I/ 100-500
CAGE, JOHN (B. 1912) AMERICAN
I/ 2420   P/ 100-1000
CAIN, CHARLES W. (1893-1962) BRITISH
I/ 100-300
CALDER, ALEXANDER STERLING (1870-1945) AMERICAN
I/ 50-18000   P/ 50-3700
CALDERARA, ANTONIO (B. 1903) ITALIAN
P/ 25-300
CALETTI, GIUSEPPE (1600-1660) ITALIAN
I/ 175-900
CALEWAERT, LOUIS (B. 1894) AMERICAN
I/ 25-100
CALLOT, JACQUES (1592-1635) FRENCH
I/ 10-25300
CAMACHO, JORGE (B. 1934) CUBAN
P 106-225
CAMARO, ALEXANDER (B. 1901) GERMAN
I/ 200   P/ 100-1000
CAMERON, SIR DAVID YOUNG (1865-1945) BRITISH
I/ 15-600
CAMOIN, CHARLES (1879-1965) FRENCH
I/ 250-350   P/ 200-350
CAMPAGNOLA, DOMENICO (1484-1550) ITALIAN
I/ 1500-17000   R/ 400-6795
CAMPENDONK, HEINRICH (1889-1957) GERMAN
R/ 60-10000
CAMPI, ANTONIO (D. 1591) ITALIAN
R/ 335-800

CAMPIGLI, MASSIMO (1895-1971) ITALIAN
I/ 1400-2400   P/ 250-2800
CANADE, VINCENT (B. 1879) AMERICAN
P/ 250
CANALETTO, (GIOVANNI ANTONIO)(1697-1768) ITALIAN
I/ 229-19500
CANCARET, JACQUES (19TH C) FRENCH
P/ 1700
CANOGAR, RAFAEL (B. 1934) SPANISH
P/ 300
CANTARINI, SIMONE (1612-1648) ITALIAN
I/ 125-7800
CANUTI, DOMENICO (1620-1684) ITALIAN
I/ 300-1600
CAPITELLI, BERNARDINO (1589-1639) ITALIAN
I/ 150-1800
CAPOGROSSI, GIUSEPPE (1900-1972) ITALIAN
P/ 150-1600   R/ 380
CAPPELLE, JAN VAN DE (1624-1679) DUTCH
I/ 800
CAPPIELLO, LEONETTO (1875-1942) ITALIAN
P/ 118-5100
CARAGLIO, GIOVANNI-JACOPO (1500-1570) ITALIAN
I/ 41-16000
CARBONELL, G. (B. 1915) FRENCH
P/ 700
CARDENAS, JUAN (B. 1939) SPANISH
I/ 725
CARDINAUX, EMILE (1877-1936) SWISS
P/ 300-4600
CARIGIET, ALOIS (B. 1902) ?
P/ 175-19000
CARISS, HENRY T. (1840-1903) AMERICAN
I/ 30-75
CARLEVARIJS, LUCA (1665-1731) ITALIAN
I/ 50-400
CARLIN, JAMES (B. 1909) AMERICAN
P/ 75-200
CARLU, JEAN (B. 1900) FRENCH
P/ 150-18000
CARO-DELAVAILLE, HENRY (1876-1926) FRENCH
P/ 3200
CARPI, UGO DA (1480-1523) ITALIAN
R/ 200-26550

CARPIONI, GIULIO (1611-1674) ITALIAN
I/ 50-2900
CARR, GEORGE (20TH C) AMERICAN
P/ 207-1540
CARRA, CARLO (1881-1966) ITALIAN
I/ 600   P/ 400-2400
CARRACCI, AGOSTINO (1557-1602) ITALIAN
I/ 100-5310
CARRACCI, ANNIBALE (1560-1609) ITALIAN
I/ 100-14000
CARRACCI, LODOVICO (1555-1619) ITALIAN
I/ 250-2600
CARRE, LEON GEORGES J. B. (1882-1962) FRENCH
P/ 400
CARRIER, AUGUSTE-JOSEPH (1800-1875) FRENCH
P/ 500
CARRIERE, EUGENE (1849-1906) FRENCH
P/ 50-2000
CARRINGTON, LEONORA (20TH C) BRITISH
P/ 500-3100
CARTER, CLARENCE HOLBROOK (B. 1904) AMERICAN
I/ 150-1200   P/ 25-880
CARTON, JEAN (B. 1912) FRENCH
I/ 50-350
CARZOU, JEAN (B. 1907) FRENCH
I/ 100-400   P/ 25-530
CASA, NICOLO DELLA (16TH C) ITALIAN
I/ 600-900
CASAS, RAMON (B. 1866) SPANISH
P/ 900-5400
CASORATI, FELICE (1886-1963) ITALIAN
I/ 2000-4000
CASPAR, KARL (1879-1956) GERMAN
P/ 50-690
CASSANDRE, A. J. M. MOURON (1901-1968) FRENCH
P/ 300-60500
CASSATT, MARY (1844-1926) AMERICAN
I/ 300-225500   P/ 6300-21000
CASSIERS, HENRY (1858-1944) BELGIAN
I/ 100-350   P/ 200-6000
CASSIGNEUL, JEAN-PIERRE (B. 1935) FRENCH
P/ 550-7500
CASTELLON, FEDERICO (1914-1971) AMERICAN
I/ 25-450   P/ 40-450

CASTIGLIONE, GIOVANNI BENEDETTO (1616-1670) ITALIAN
I/ 160-8200
CASTIGLIONE, GUISEPPE (1829-1908) ITALIAN
I/ 125-518000
CASTILLO, JORGE (B. 1933) SPANISH
I/ 75-3500   P/ 426
CATLIN, GEORGE (1796-1872) AMERICAN
P/ 200-9400
CAULAERT, JEAN DOMINIQUE VAN (20TH C) FRENCH
P/ 150-3600
CAULFIELD, PATRICK (B. 1936) BRITISH
P/ 25-1000
CAVAEL, ROLF (B. 1898) GERMAN
P/ 100-1400
CAVALLIERI, GIOVANNI BATTISTA (1525-1597) ITALIAN
I/ 100-3200
CAZALS, FREDERIC A. (1865-1941) FRENCH
P/ 200-5200
CEMINS, VIJA (B. 1939) AMERICAN
P/ 450-600
CESAR, (B. 1921) FRENCH
I/ 560   P/ 30-950
CEZANNE, PAUL (1839-1906) FRENCH
I/ 100-13200   P/ 200-79750
CHADWICK, LYNN (B. 1914) BRITISH
P/ 50-1250
CHAGALL, MARC (1887-1985) RUSSIAN/FRENCH
I/ 100-77400   P/ 25-99000   R/ 800-50000
CHAHINE, EDGAR (1874-1947) FRENCH
I/ 55-8000
CHAKA, FRANK (B. 1887) AMERICAN
I/ 25-100
CHAMBERLAIN, PRICE A. (B. 1905) AMERICAN
R/ 25-100
CHAMBERLAIN, SAMUEL (1895-1975) AMERICAN
I/ 50-800
CHANDLER, GEORGE W. (20TH C) AMERICAN
I/ 25-100
CHAPELLIER, PH. (20TH C) ?
P/ 375-2200
CHAPIN, JAMES ORMSBEE (1887-1975) AMERICAN
P/ 175
CHAPLIN, PRESCOTT (1897-1968) AMERICAN
R/ 50-125

CHARBONNIER, LOUISE (20TH C) FRENCH
P/ 1000-2000
CHARLET, NICOLAS T. (1792-1845) FRENCH
P/ 75-1400
CHARLOT, JEAN (1898-1979) AMERICAN
P/ 75-400
CHASE, LOUISA (B. 1951) AMERICAN
R/ 800-2700   P/ 500-600
CHASE, WILLIAM MERRITT (1849-1916) AMERICAN
I/ 75-1210   P/ 4950-5500
CHASSERIAU, THEODORE (1819-1856) FRENCH
P/ 50-1200
CHASTEL, ROGER (1897-1981) FRENCH
I/ 50
CHAVANNES, PIERRE (19TH/20TH C) FRENCH
P/ 400
CHAVIGNIERE, LOUIS (1922-1972) FRENCH
I/ 2100
CHEFFER, HENRY (B. 1880) FRENCH
I/ 25-200
CHEFFETZ, ASA (1896-1965) AMERICAN
R/ 75-880
CHENEY, PHILIP (B. 1897) AMERICAN
P/ 75-250
CHERET, JULES (1836-1932) FRENCH
P/ 40-7700
CHERRY, EDWARD J. (20TH C) BRITISH
I/ 25-100
CHEVILLET, JUSTE (1729-1790) FRENCH
I/ 800
CHIA, SANDRO (B. 1946) ITALIAN
I/ 400-2000   P/ 1000-7700
CHIARI, FABRIZIO (1621-1695) ITALIAN
I/ 200-825
CHICAGO, JUDY (B. 1939) AMERICAN
P/ 300-500
CHILDS, BERNARD (B. 1910) AMERICAN
I/ 150
CHILLIDA, EDUARDO (B. 1924) SPANISH
I/ 30-3700   P/ 100-1700   R/ 150-1500
CHIMOT, EDOUARD (20TH C) FRENCH
I/ 50-270
CHIRICO, GIORGIO DE (1888-1978) ITALIAN
I/ 600-3600   P/ 50-9700

CHODOWIECKI, DANIEL (1726-1801) GERMAN
I/ 50-3200
CHOUBRAC, ALFRED (1853-1902) FRENCH
P/ 100-2200
CHRISTIANSEN, NILS HANS (1873-1960) DANISH
P/ 3200
CHRISTO, (CHRISTO JAVACHEFF) (B. 1935) AMER/BULGARIAN
P/ 100-22000
CIRY, MICHEL (B. 1919) FRENCH
I/ 50-500
CISSARZ, JOHANN (1873-1942) GERMAN
P/ 150-2000
CITRON, MINNA (1896-1992) AMERICAN
P/ 150-500
CLAESZ, ALLAERT (17TH C) DUTCH
I/ 600-2400
CLAPP, WILLIAM HENRY (1879-1954) AMERICAN
I/ 385   P/ 450
CLARENBACH, MAX (1880-1952) GERMAN
I/ 100-1900   P/ 250
CLAUSEN, GEORGE (1852-1944) BRITISH
I/ 100-300
CLAVE, ANTONI (B. 1913) SPANISH
I/ 10-2300   P/ 75-3600
CLEMENTE, FRANCESCO (B. 1952) SPANISH
I/ 175-13000   P/ 150-19800   R/ 375-11000
CLOSE, CHUCK (B. 1940) AMERICAN
I/ 80-11550   P/ 3000-16000   R/ 3300-33000
CLOUWET, PEETER (1629-1670) FLEMISH
I/ 800
COCHIN, CHARLES NICOLAS (1715-1790) FRENCH
I/ 300-4500
COCK, HIERONYMUS (1510-1570) FLEMISH
I/ 175-5100   R/ 882
COCK, JAN WELLENS (1480-1526) FLEMISH
R/ 2700
COCLERS, J.B.B. (1741-1817) FLEMISH
I/ 1800
COCTEAU, JEAN (1889-1963) FRENCH
I/ 50-460   P/ 65-13200
COESTER, OTTO (B. 1902) GERMAN
I/ 25-100
COK, ZLATANA (20TH C) ?
I/ 30-125

Technique Key

Under each <u>printing technique</u> you may encounter the following types of prints (or combination of processes):

- **I** <u>Intaglio:</u>
  - etching
  - drypoint
  - steel engraving
  - stipple engraving
  - aquatint
  - mezzotint
  - soft-ground etching
  - crayon manner

- **P** <u>Planographic:</u>
  - lithograph
  - monotype
  - silk-screen
  - cliche verre
  - serigraph

- **R** <u>Relief:</u>
  - wood block
    - woodcut
      - chiaroscuro
    - wood engraving
  - linoleum cut (linocut)

COIGNARD, JAMES (B. 1925) FRENCH
I/ 75-1700   P/ 690
COLEMAN, GLENN O. (1887-1932) AMERICAN
P/ 550-4700
COLIN, PAUL EMILE (1892-1984) FRENCH
P/ 50-13200   R/ 25-200
COLLAERT, ADRIAEN (1560-1618) FLEMISH
I/ 50-900
COLLAERT, HANS I/ (16TH C) FLEMISH
I/ 200-500
COLLIEN, PETER (20TH C) ?
I/ 50-250
COLQUHOUN, ROBERT (20TH C) ?
P/ 664-2000
COLVILLE, ALEX (B. 1920) CANADIAN
P/ 2700
COMBA, PAUL (B. 1926) FRENCH
P/ 400
COMBAZ, GISBERT (B. 1869) BELGIAN
P/ 500-7000
COMMARMOND, PIERRE (20TH C) FRENCH
P/ 225-550
CONGDON, THOMAS R. (1862-1917) AMERICAN
I/ 25-100
CONSTABLE, JOHN (1776-1837) BRITISH
I/ 150-5200
CONTE, ANTONIO (1780-1837) ITALIAN
I/ 800
CONZ, WALTER (B. 1872) GERMAN
I/ 75-200   P/ 75-150
COOGHEN, LEENDERT VAN DER (1610-1681) DUTCH
I/ 400-2400
COOK, HOWARD (1901-1980) AMERICAN
I/ 150-6600   P/ 100-6600   R/ 200-3850
COOPER, AUSTIN (B. 1890) CANADIAN
P/ 200-4000
COORNHERT, DIRK (1522-1590) DUTCH
I/ 125-1600
COPLEY, JOHN (1875-1950) BRITISH
P/ 25-1500
CORBUSIER, LE (1887-1965) FRENCH
I/ 90-4500   P/ 250-7300   R/ 625
CORINTH, LOVIS (1858-1925) GERMAN
I/ 25-8500   P/ 25-8700   R/ 300-1200

CORIOLANO, BARTOLOMEO (1599-1676) ITALIAN
R/ 200-4100
CORNEILLE, (CORNELIUS G. B.) (B. 1922) DUTCH
I/ 300-700   P/ 25-3600   R/ 150-1000
CORNELL, JOSEPH (1903-1972) AMERICAN
I/ 300   P/ 1000-3300
CORNELL, THOMAS (B. 1937) AMERICAN
I/ 25-100
COROT, JEAN BAPTISTE CAMILLE (1796-1875) FRENCH
I/ 175-15000   P/ 50-15000
CORPORA, ANTONIO (B. 1909) ITALIAN
P/ 100-250
CORRELL, RICHARD (B. 1904) AMERICAN
P 25-100
CORT, CORNELIS (1533-1578) DUTCH
I/ 150-9500
COSTIGAN, JOHN EDWARD (1888-1972) AMERICAN
I/ 88-300
COTTINGHAM, ROBERT (B. 1935) AMERICAN
I/ 125-500   P/ 200-1100
COUDREY, R. DU (19TH/20TH C) FRENCH
P/ 500-600
COUGHLIN, JACK (B. 1932) AMERICAN
I/ 10-75
COULTER, MARY J. (1880-1966) AMERICAN
R/ 1800
COURBET, GUSTAVE (1819-1877) FRENCH
P/ 275-1000
COURTOIS, GUSTAVE CLAUDE ETIENNE (1853-1923) FRENCH
I/ 350   P/ 450
COUSSENS, ARMAND (1881-1935) FRENCH
I/ 50-200
COUTAUD, LUCIEN (1904-1977) FRENCH
I/ 200-300   P/ 50-300
COWIN, JACK (20TH C) ?
P/ 200-300
COX, CHARLES BRINTON (1864-1905) AMERICAN
P/ 800
CRAIG, EDWARD G. (1872-1966) BRITISH
I/ 50   R/ 11-1100
CRANACH, LUCAS I (1472-1553) GERMAN
I/ 1100-13200   R/ 125-75000
CRANACH, LUCAS II (1515-1586) GERMAN
R/ 200-500

CRAWFORD, RALSTON (1906-1978) AMERICAN
P/ 330-38500   R/ 3000
CREMER, FRITZ (B. 1906) ?
P/ 50-100
CREMONINI, LEONARDO (B. 1925) ITALIAN
I/ 300
CROME, JOHN (1768-1821) BRITISH
I/ 25-250
CRESPIN, ADOLPHE (B. 1859) BELGIAN
P/ 300-5500
CRODEL, CHARLES (1894-1973) FRENCH
P/ 100-1800   R/ 475-2000
CROSS (DELACROIX), HENRI EDMOND (1856-1910) FRENCH
P/ 300-16000
CROTTI, JEAN (1878-1958) FRENCH
P/ 300-700
CRUTCHFIELD, WILLIAM (B. 1932) AMERICAN
P/ 50-450
CRUZ-DIEZ, CARLOS (B. 1923) VENEZUELAN
P/ 250
CUCCHI, ENZO (B. 1950) ITALIAN
I/ 600-18000   P/ 605-3300
CUEVAS, JOSE LUIS (B. 1934) MEXICAN/AMERICAN
I/ 150   P/ 75 900
CUITT, GEORGE (THE YOUNGER) (1779-1854) BRITISH
I/ 300-375
CUNEGO, DOMENICO (1727-1794) ITALIAN
I/ 200-250
CUNNINGHAM, W. PHELPS (1904-1980) AMERICAN
I/ 75-200
CURRY, JOHN STEUART (1897-1946) AMERICAN
P/ 200-6325
CURTI, BERNARDINO (B. 1645) ITALIAN
I/ 150

D

D'ARCANGELO, ALLAN (B. 1930) AMERICAN
P/ 500-900
DAHL, PETER (B. 1934) SWEDISH

P/ 1000-2000
DAHLGREEN, CHARLES W. (1864-1955) AMERICAN
   I/ 40-100
DAHM, HELEN (B. 1878) GERMAN
   I/ 212   P/ 200-1500   R/ 1100
DAHMEN, KARL FRED (B. 1917) AMERICAN
   I/ 25-10000   P/ 100-1000
DALEN, CORNELIS VAN (1602-1665) DUTCH
   I/ 150-1000
DALEN, CORNELIS II (1638-1664) DUTCH
   I/ 300-1100
DALI, SALVADOR (1904-1989)) SPANISH
   I/ 25-8800   P/ 50-10240   R/ 55-800
DALLMAN, DANIEL (B. 1942) AMERICAN
   I/ 30-125
DANIEL, LEWIS C. (1901-1952) AMERICAN
   I/ 20-75
DASKALOFF, GEORGE (B. 1923) BULGARIAN
   P/ 75-125
DAUBIGNY, CHARLES FRANCOIS (1817-1878) FRENCH
   I/ 40-1200   P/ 100-2500
DAUMIER, HONORE (1808-1879) FRENCH
   P/ 25-28000
DAVENT, LEON (16TH C) FRENCH
   I/ 200-6300
DAVIE, ALAN (B. 1920) BRITISH
   P/ 100-1500
DAVIES, ARTHUR BOWEN (1862-1928) AMERICAN
   I/ 125-4100   P/ 150-550
DAVIS, GENE (B. 1920) AMERICAN
   P/ 130-600
DAVIS, RONALD (RON) WENDELL (B. 1937) AMERICAN
   I/ 100-525   P/ 125-1500
DAVIS, STUART (1894-1964) AMERICAN
   P/ 275-19000
DAVIS, WARREN B. (1865-1928) AMERICAN
   I/ 50-250
DAVIS, WILLIAM S. (1884-1959) AMERICAN
   I/ 25-100   R/ 25-100
DAVRINGHAUSEN, HENRI DARVING (B. 1900) GERMAN
   P/ 100-450
DEBUCOURT, PHILIBERT LOUIS (1755-1832) FRENCH
   I/ 175-22000
DECORDOBA, MATHILDE (1875-1942) AMERICAN

I/ 25-100
DEFAU, CLEMENTINE (19TH/20TH C) ?
P/ 4000
DEGAS, EDGAR (1834-1917) FRENCH
I/ 100-204000   P/ 700-551000
DEHN, ADOLPH ARTHUR (1895-1968) AMERICAN
P/ 25-770
DEHNER, DOROTHY (B. 1908) AMERICAN
I/ 75-1650
DEINEKA, ALEXANDER (B. 1899) RUSSIAN
P/ 600
DEINES, ERNEST HUBERT (1894-1967) AMERICAN
R/ 220
DELACROIX, EUGENE (1798-1863) FRENCH
I/ 50-16000   P/ 75-33000
DELARUE-NOUVELLIER (20TH C) FRENCH
P/ 1200
DELATRE, EUGENE (1864-1938) FRENCH
I/ 50-1500
DELAUNAY, ROBERT (1885-1941) FRENCH
P/ 75-57000
DELAUNAY, SONIA (1885-1979) RUSSIAN/FRENCH
I/ 150-3400   P/ 90-13000
DELTEIL, LOYS (1869-1927) FRENCH
I/ 200
DELVAUX, PAUL (B. 1897) BELGIAN
I/ 200-10000   P/ 75-36000
DE MARTELLY, JOHN STOCKTON (B. 1903)
P/ 80-600
DEMARTEAU, GILLES (1722-1776) FRENCH
I/ 100-12000
DENIS, MAURICE (1870-1943) FRENCH
I/ 100-400   P/ 100-14400   R/ 25-11000
DENNIS, MORGAN (1892-1960) AMERICAN
I/ 50-125
DENON, DOMINIQUE V. (1747-1825) FRENCH
I/ 200-550   P/ 200-900
DENTE, MARCO (D. 1527) ITALIAN
I/ 75-8000
DERAIN, ANDRE (1880-1954) FRENCH
I/ 25-4700   P/ 50-3000   R/ 100-7900
DESBOUTIN, MARCELIN (1823-1902) FRENCH
I/ 200-300
DESCOURTIS, CHARLES-MELCHOIR (1753-1820) FRENCH

I/ 200-7800
DESNOYER, FRANCOIS (1894-1972) FRENCH
P/ 80-170
DETHOMAS, MAXIME (1867-1929) FRENCH
P/ 1200
DETMOLD, CHARLES MAURICE (1883-1908) BRITISH
and
DETMOLD, EDWARD J. (1883-1957) BRITISH
I/ 100-3000
DETOUCHE, HENRY (1854-1913) FRENCH
I/ 110-600   P/ 100-1000
DEUTSCH, ERNST (B. 1883) AUSTRIAN
P/ 175-3520
DEXEL, WALTER (1890-1973) GERMAN
P/ 100-1200   R/ 300-2200
DEYROLLE, JEAN (1911-1967) FRENCH
I/ 152   P/ 150-450
DEYSTER, LUDWIG VAN (1656-1711) GERMAN
I/ 100-1200
DIACRE, JEAN DOMINIQUE (17TH/18TH C) FRENCH
I/ 50
DICHTL, MARTIN (17TH C) GERMAN
I/ 24-2500
DICKINSON, WILLIAM (1746-1767) BRITISH
I/ 200
DICKSEE, HERBERT (1862-1942) BRITISH
I/ 100-400
DIEBENKORN, RICHARD (1922-1993) AMERICAN
I/ 450-113800   P/ 650-66000   R/ 2750-44100
DIES, ALBERT C. (1755-1822) AUSTRIAN
I/ 100-200
DIETRICH, CHRISTIAN WILHELM ERNST (1712-1774) GERMAN
I/ 25-3800   R/ 250-1000
DIEZ, JULIUS (B. 1870) GERMAN
P/ 189-1000
DIGGELMANN, ALEX W.
P/ 300-3100
DIGHTON, ROBERT (1752-1812) BRITISH
I/ 250
DILL, LADDIE JOHN
P/ 250-1000
DILL, OTTO (1884-1957) GERMAN
P/ 19-300
DINE, JIM (B. 1935) AMERICAN

Technique Key

Under each <u>printing technique</u> you may encounter the following types of prints (or combination of processes):

- **I** <u>Intaglio:</u>
  - etching
  - drypoint
  - steel engraving
  - stipple engraving
  - aquatint
  - mezzotint
  - soft-ground etching
  - crayon manner

- **P** <u>Planographic:</u>
  - lithograph
  - monotype
  - silk-screen
  - cliche verre
  - serigraph

- **R** <u>Relief:</u>
  - wood block
    - woodcut
      - chiaroscuro
    - wood engraving
  - linoleum cut (linocut)

I/ 100-45100   P/ 50-41000   R/ 75-42000
DISTLER, RUDOLPH ?
    I/ 100-450
DITTRICH, SIMON ?
    I/ 80-300   P/ 25-100
DIX, OTTO (1891-1969) GERMAN
    I/ 300-28500   P/ 50-50400   R/ 100-14000
DIXON, FREDERICK C. (B. 1902) BRITISH
    I/ 100-300
DOBKIN, ALEXANDER (1908-1975) ITALIAN
    P/ 6-75
DOBSON, FRANK (1888-1963) BRITISH
    P/ 600
DODD, FRANCIS (1874-1949) BRITISH
    I/ 100-700
DODEIGNE, EUGENE (B. 1923) FRENCH
    P/ 200
DODGE, OZIAS (1868-1925) AMERICAN
    I/ 25-100
DOESER, JACOB (1623-1673) ITALIAN
    P/ 1200
DOHANOS, STEVAN (B. 1907) AMERICAN
    P/ 150-440   R/ 100-450
DOLICE, LEON (1892-1960) AMERICAN
    I/ 50-125
DOMELA, CESAR (B. 1900) DUTCH
    P/ 75-550   R/ 510
DOMENJOZ, RAOUL (B. 1896) SWISS
    P/ 200
DOMERGUE, JEAN GABRIEL (1889-1962) FRENCH
    I/ 300-650   P/ 100-2500
DOMINGUEZ, OSCAR (1906-1958) SPANISH
    I/ 800   P/ 75-955
DOMJAN, JOSEPH (B. 1907) AMERICAN
    R/ 50-825
DONGEN, KEES VAN (1877-1968) DUTCH/FRENCH
    I/ 150-500   P/ 25-7200
DONNAY, AUGUSTE (1862-1921) BELGIAN
    P/ 450-700
DOOLITTLE, HAROLD LUKENS (20TH C) AMERICAN
    I/ 100-450
DORAZIO, PIERO (B. 1927) ITALIAN
    I/ 75-1000   P/ 150-800
DORIVAL, GEORGES (B. 1879) FRENCH

P/ 300-1000
DORN, LEO F. (B. 1879) AMERICAN
R/ 50-125
DORNY, BERTRAND (B. 1931) FRENCH
I/ 125-500
DOUGLAS, LUCILLE (D. 1935) AMERICAN
I/ 25-100
DOW, ARTHUR WESLEY (1857-1922) AMERICAN
R/ 50-12000
DRESSLER, AUGUST W. (20TH C) ?
I/ 100-1800   P/ 2250
DREWES, WERNER (1899-1985) AMERICAN
I/ 300-1000   P/ 303   R/ 50-1500
DRIAN, A. (20TH C) FRENCH
I/ 75-350
DROIT, JEAN (20TH C) FRENCH
P/ 2400-4400
DROOCHSLOOT, JOOST CORNELISZ (1586-1666) DUTCH
I/ 2900
DRURY, PAUL (1903-1988) BRITISH
I/ 400-475
DRURY, WILLIAM (1888-1959) AMERICAN
I/ 25-100
DUBUFFET, JEAN (1901-1985) FRENCH
I/ 500-1300   P/ 5-88000   R/ 200-2400
DUCHAMP, MARCEL (1887-1968) FRENCH/AMERICAN
I/ 200-8500   P/ 50-9700   R/ 12000
DUCHAMP, SUZANNA (1898-1963) FRENCH
I/ 27   P/ 175-500
DUCK, JACOB (1600-1667) DUTCH
I/ 200-1000
DUDOVICH, MARCELLO (B. 1878) ITALIAN
P/ 400-18000
DUFAU, CLEMENTINE (B. 1869) FRENCH
P/ 900-9000
DUFRESNE, CHARLES (1876-1938) FRENCH
P/ 400-850
DUFY, RAOUL (1877-1953) FRENCH
I/ 40-3550   P/ 90-6400   R/ 75-8100
DUJARDIN, KAREL (1622-1678) DUTCH
I/ 25-400
DUNCAN, RAYMOND (20TH C) BRITISH
R/ 75-200
DUNKER, BALTHASAR ANTON (1746-1807) GERMAN

I/ 950
DUNOYER DE SEGONZAC, ANDRE (1884-1974) FRENCH
    I/ 75-5500
DUPAS, JEAN THEODORE (1882-1964) FRENCH
    I/ 500-7700   P/ 600-19250
DUPUIS, EDMOND-MARIE (20TH C) FRENCH
    I/ 350
DURER, ALBRECHT (1471-1528) GERMAN
    I/ 100-512000   R/ 25-167587
DUSAMANTES, FRANCISCO (20TH C) AMERICAN
    P/ 100-300
DUSART, CORNELIUS (1660-1704) DUTCH
    I/ 175-20600
DUTHE, J. (19TH C) FRENCH
    I/ 100-400
DUVENECK, FRANK (1848-1919) AMERICAN
    I/ 990-3300
DUVET, JEAN (1485-1570) FRENCH
    I/ 3600-115000
DUVIVIER, IGNACE (1758-1832) FRENCH
    I/ 200-300
DWIGHT, MABEL (1876-1955) AMERICAN
    P/ 75-700
DYCK, SIR ANTHONY VAN (1599-1641) FLEMISH
    I/ 150-65000
DZUBAS, FRIEDEL (B. 1915) GERMAN/AMERICAN
    P/ 700-9350

E

EAMES, JOHN H. (B. 1900) AMERICAN
    I/ 25-100
EARLOM, RICHARD (1743-1822) BRITISH
    I/ 150-2300
EBERZ, JOSEF (B. 1880) GERMAN
    I/ 50-1300   P/ 25-500   R/ 25-580
EBY, KERR (1889-1946) AMERICAN
    I/ 40-3300   P/ 80-440
EDEL, EDMUND (B. 1863) GERMAN
    P/ 500-1200

EDELMANN, YRJO (B. 1941) FINNISH
P/ 75-225
EDZARD, DIETZ (1893-1963) GERMAN
I/ 250
EGGENSCHWILER, FRANZ (B. 1930) SWISS
R/ 100-3200
EGGERS, GEORGE WILLIAM (1883-1958) AMERICAN
P/ 50-125
EGGIMANN, HANS (B. 1872) SWISS
I/ 150
EGLAU, OTTO (B. 1917) GERMAN
I/ 64-900
EHMSEN, HEINRICH
I/ 100-900   P/ 335   R/ 100-800
EHRLICH, GEORG (1897-1966) AUSTRIAN
I/ 100-700   P/ 150-400
EICHENBERG, FRITZ (B. 1901) AMERICAN
R/ 50-1000
EISEN, CHARLES DOMINIQUE JOSEPH (1720-1778) FRENCH
I/ 400-700
ELIASBERG, PAUL (B. 1907) GERMAN
I/ 50-600
ELZINGRE, EDOUARD (20TH C) SWISS)
P/ 800-2600
ENDE, EDGAR (1901-1965) GERMAN
I/ 225-1300   P/ 150-1000
ENDE, HANS AM (1864-1918) GERMAN
I/ 150-1900
ENDELL, FRITZ (B. 1873) AMERICAN
R/ 25-100
ENGEL, JULES (B. 1915)
P/ 450
ENGELBRECHT, MARTIN (1684-1756) GERMAN
I/ 600-12000
ENGELHARDT, PAUL (?) ?
P/ 800-2000
ENSOR, JAMES (1860-1949) BELGIAN
I/ 80-19400   P/ 125-5400
ERBSLOH, ADOLF (1881-1947) GERMAN
P/ 275-1200
ERDT, HANS RUDI ?
P/ 200-2600
ERHARD, JOHANN C. (1795-1822) GERMAN
I/ 75-800

ERLER, ERICH ?
I/ 25-200   P/ 400-1200
ERLER, GEORG (B. 1871) GERMAN
I/ 150-250
ERNI, HANS (B. 1909) SWISS
I/ 75-1800   P/ 25-3200
ERNST, MAX (1891-1976) FRENCH
I/ 150-70000   P/ 20-18000   R/ 166
ERRO, GUDMUNDUR (B. 1932) ICELANDIC
P/ 100-875
ERTE, (ROMAIN DE TIRTOFF) (1892-1990) RUSSIAN
P/ 125-5500
ERTZ, EDWARD F. (1862-1954) AMERICAN
I/ 25-100
ESCHER, MAURITS CORNELIS (1898-1972) DUTCH
I/ 700-10000   P/ 200-37000   R/ 150-77000
ESCHER, ROLF (RUDOLF) (1662-1721) SWISS
I/ 125
ESTEBY, J.M. (20TH C) AMERICAN
I/ 75-150
ESTES, RICHARD (B. 1936) AMERICAN
P/ 600-16000
ESTEVE, MAURICE (B. 1904) FRENCH
I/ 1000-3000   P/ 175-8700
ETTINGER, CHURCHILL (1903-1985) AMERICAN
I/ 40-125
EVENEPOEL, HENRI (1872-1899) BELGIAN
P/ 700-2200
EVERDINGEN, ALLART VAN (1621-1675) DUTCH
I/ 29-3000
EVERGOOD, PHILIP (1901-1973) AMERICAN
I/ 99   P 100-440
EXTER, ALEXANDRA (1884-1949) RUSSIAN
P/ 350-400

F

FABER, WILL (?) ?
P/ 100-300
FABRI, RALPH (1894-1975) AMERICAN

I/ 25 -125
FACCINI, PIETRO (1562-1602) ITALIAN
    I/ 400-2400
FAIVRE, JULES ABEL (1867-1945) FRENCH
    P/ 850-4200
FALCK, JEREMIAS (1619-1677) ?
    I/ 100-2400
FALCONE, ANIELLO (1607-1656) ITALIAN
    I/ 400-1100
FALDONI, GIOVANNI (1690-1770) ITALIAN
    I/ 200-300
FALK, HANS (?) ?
    P/ 175-2100
FANTIN-LATOUR, IGNACE HENRI J. T. (1836-1904) FRENCH
    I/ 346   P/ 25-2200
FANTUZZI, ANTONIO (16TH C) ITALIAN
    I/ 1200-21000
FARINATI, ORAZIO (1559-1616) ITALIAN
    I/ 40-1100
FARINATI, PAOLO (1524-1606) ITALIAN
    I/ 250-3850
FARLEY, FREDERICK (B. 1895) AMERICAN
    I/ 30-125
FASSBENDER, JOSEPH (B. 1903) GERMAN
    I/ 193   P/ 125-3700
FATHWINTER, F.A. TH. (B. 1906) GERMAN
    P/ 250
FAURE, LUCIEN (1828-1904) FRENCH
    P/ 300-900
FAUTRIER, JEAN (1898-1964) FRENCH
    I/ 125-7400   P/ 350-2000
FEININGER, LYONEL (1871-1956) AMERICAN
    I/ 600-17600   P/ 700-8200   R/ 100-19000
FEKETE, ESTEBAN (B. 1924)
    I/ 225   P/ 250   R/ 50-500
FELBER, CARL FRIEDRICH (1880-1932) SWISS
    I/ 250   P/ 300
FELDMAN, WALTER (B. 1925) AMERIACAN
    R/ 25-100
FELIXMULLER, CONRAD (1897-1977) GERMAN
    I/ 200-8000   P/ 100-58000   R/ 25-19000
FENNEKER, JOSEPH (?) ?
    P/ 1900-10000
FENNITZER, GEORG (17TH C) GERMAN

Technique Key

Under each <u>printing technique</u> you may encounter the following types of prints (or combination of processes):

- **I** <u>Intaglio:</u>
  - etching
  - drypoint
  - steel engraving
  - stipple engraving
  - aquatint
  - mezzotint
  - soft-ground etching
  - crayon manner

- **P** <u>Planographic:</u>
  - lithograph
  - monotype
  - silk-screen
  - cliche verre
  - serigraph

- **R** <u>Relief:</u>
  - wood block
    - woodcut
      - chiaroscuro
    - wood engraving
  - linoleum cut (linocut)

I/ 200
FENTON, JOHN WILLIAM (1875-1939) AMERICAN
I/ 125
FERGUSON, EDWARD R. (B. 1914) AMERICAN
P/ 25-100
FERNEL ?
P/ 150-5000
FETTING, RAINER (B. 1949) GERMAN
I/ 700-4000   P/ 1900-2500
FEURE, GEORGES DE (1868-1943) FRENCH
P/ 150-10000
FIALETTI, ODOARDO (1573-1638) ITALIAN
I/ 150-6200
FIENE, ERNEST (1894-1965) AMERICAN
I/ 125-900   P/ 80-1300
FILMUS, TULLY (B.1908) AMERICAN
P/ 40-125
FINCKEN, JAMES H. (1860-1943) AMERICAN
I/ 50-100
FINDLAY, ANNE (20TH C) AMERICAN
R/ 30-100
FINGESTEN, MICHAEL (1884-1946) ?
I/ 75-550   P/ 100-400
FINI, LEONOR (B. 1918) ARGENTINIAN
I/ 50-1400   P/ 110-900
FIORINI, MARCEL (B. 1922) FRENCH
I/ 100-600
FISCHER, CLEMENS
I/ 200-350
FISCHL, ERIC (B. 1948) AMERICAN
I/ 150-14000   P/ 3200-9000   R/ 2336
FISH, JANET (B. 1938) AMERICAN
R/ 1540-1600
FIX-MASSEAU, PIERRE (1869-1937) FRENCH
P/ 500-13000
FLACK, AUDREY (B. 1931) AMERICAN
P/ 50-350
FLAMEN, ALBERT (17TH C) FLEMISH
I/ 75-300
FLANAGAN, ALBERT (B. 1886) AMERAICAN
I/ 25-100
FLEISCHMANN, ADOLF (1892-1969) GERMAN
P/ 150-1000
FLETCHER, F. MORLEY (1866-1949) BRITISH/AMERICAN

R/ 400-900
FLIGHT, CLAUDE (1881-1955) BRITISH
R/ 50-18000
FLINT, SIR WILLIAM RUSSELL (1880-1969) BRITISH
I/ 100-1500   P/ 200-4000
FLIPART, JEAN-JACQUES (1719-1782) FRENCH
I/ 800
FLORIS, FRANS (1516-1570) FLEMISH
I/ 300-1600
FLORSHEIM, RICHARD (1916-1979) AMERICAN
P/ 50-125
FOLON, JEAN MICHEL (B. 1934) BELGIAN
I/ 220-1100   P/ 50-1600
FONTANA, GIOVANNI BATTISTA (1524-1587) ?
I/ 400-4300
FONTANA, LUCIO (1899-1968) ITALIAN
I/ 100-4675   P/ 250-6100   R/ 5237
FONTEBASSO, FRANCESCO (1709-1769) ITALIAN
I/ 600-5840
FORAIN, JEAN LOUIS (1852-1931) FRENCH
I/ 35-2000   P/ 80-2200
FOREST, ROY DEAN DE (B. 1930) AMERICAN
P/ 200-850
FORTUNY Y CARBO, MARIANO (1838-1874) SPANISH
I/ 250-2800
FOULKES, LYN (20TH C) AMERICAN
P/ 75-175
FOUJITA, TSUGUHARU LEONARD (1886-1968) JAPANESE
I/ 100-46800   P/ 60-48000   R/ 150-6600
FOWLER, FRANK (1852-1910) AMERICAN
I/ 25-100
FRAME, WALTER (B. 1895) AMERICAN
I/ 20-80
FRANCIA, JACOPO (1487-1557) ITALIAN
I/ 500-10000
FRANCIS, SAM (B. 1923) AMERICAN
I/ 500-29000   P/ 200-83600   R/ 15000-21000
FRANCK, PHILIPP (1860-1944) GERMAN
I/ 100-400
FRANCKSEN, JEAN E. (B. 1914) AMERIACAN
P/ 25-100
FRANCO, GIOVANNI BATTISTA (1510-1580) ITALIAN
I/ 200-3500
FRANK, HANS (1884-1959) GERMAN

Important: For an explanation of I, P, and R see pages 16-28 and 45-47

I/ 350   R/ 100-300
FRANK, MARY (B. 1933) AMERICAN
I/ 700-1320   P/ 400-2500
FRANK, SEPP (?) ?
I/ 25-700
FRANKENTHALER, HELEN (B. 1928) AMERICAN
I/ 1100-52250   P/ 50-42840   R/ 3500-44000
FRASCONI, ANTONIO M. (B. 1919) AMERICAN
P/ 220   R/ 25-900
FREDERICK, FRANK FOREST (B. 1866) AMERICAN
R/ 200
FREEDMAN, LOUISE A. (B. 1915) AMERICAN
P/ 50-200
FREEMAN, DON (1908-1978) AMERICAN
P/ 75-900
FREEMAN, MARK (B. 1908) AMERICAN
P/ 100-935
FRELAUT, JEAN (1879-1954) FRENCH
I/ 150-2500
FRESNAYE, ROGER DE LA (1885-1925) FRENCH
P/ 75-1500
FREUD, LUCIEN (B. 1922) BRITISH
I/ 275-32000
FREUNDLICH, OTTO (1878-1943) GERMAN
R/ 100 1543
FRIDELL, AXEL (1894-1935) ?
I/ 450-9600
FRIEDLAENDER, JULIUS (1810-1861) DANISH
I/ 80-3700   P/ 80-700
FRIEDLANDER, ISAC (1890-1968) AMERICAN
I/ 200   R/ 100-250
FRIEDLANDER, JOHNNY (B. 1912) GERMAN
P/ 80-800
FRIEDRICH, ADOLF (1750-1803) SWEDISH
I/ 150-700
FRIEDRICH, CASPAR DAVID (1774-1840) GERMAN
I/ 400-62000   R/ 1835
FRIES, ERNST (1801-1833) GERMAN
P/ 75-4000
FRIESZ, ACHILLE EMILE OTHON (1879-1949) FRENCH
I/ 100-500   P/ 25-1200   R/ 50-300
FRINK, ELIZABETH (B. 1930) BRITISH
I/ 25-330   P/ 40-1100
FRISCHMANN, MARCEL

I/ 150-300
FRITZSCH, CHRISTIAN F. (1695-1747) DUTCH
  I/ 950
FROHNER, ADOLF (B. 1934) AUSTRIAN
  I/ 25-350   P/ 475
FRUHTRUNK, GUENTER (B. 1923) GERMAN
  P/ 100-800
FRY, ROWENA (20TH C) AMERICAN
  P/ 25-75
FUCHS, ERNST (B. 1930) AUSTRIAN
  I/ 25-6000   P/ 75-1200
FUHR, ERNEST (1874-1933) AMERICAN
  I/ 25-100   P/ 25-100
FULLER, ALFRED (B. 1899) AMERICAN
  P/ 25-100
FULLER, BUCKMINISTER
  I/ 150-4000
FUSS, ALBERT (?) ?
  P/ 150-8000
FUSSMANN, KLAUS (B. 1938) GERMAN
  I/ 25-800   P/ 150-400

G

GABAIN, ETHEL (1883-1950) BRITISH
  P/ 200-1500
GABO, NAUM (1890-1977) AMERICAN/BRITISH
  P/ 1460   R/ 2000-11000
GACHET, PAUL F. (1828-1929) FRENCH
  I/ 500-1500
GACHNANG, JOHANNES (B. 1939) SWISS
  I/ 50-300
GAG, WANDA (1893-1946) AMERICAN
  P/ 200-450
GAILLARD, EMMANUEL (20TH C) FRENCH
  P/ 800-1300
GALE, GEORGE (8193-1951) AMERICAN
  I/ 50-100
GALESTRUSSI, GIOVANNI-BATTISTA (1615-1669) ITALIAN
  I/ 500-750

GALLAGHER, MICHAEL J. (1898-1965) AMERICAN
P/ 25-100   R/ 25-100
GALLAGHER, SEARS (1869-1955) AMERICAN
I/ 75-400   P/ 50-150
GALLAND, A.
P/ 200-1100
GALLE, CORNELIS (1576-1650) DUTCH
I/ 150-1000
GALLE, PHILIPPE (1537-1629) DUTCH
I/ 25-2300
GALLE, THEODOR (1571-1633) DUTCH
I/ 250-1000
GALLI, RICCARDO (B. 1839) ITALIAN
P/ 990
GALLICE, A. (19TH C) MEXICAN
P/ 275
GANDINI, ALESSANDRO (active 1550-1600) ITALIAN
R/ 650-4300
GANGOLF, PAUL
I/ 200-400   P/ 100-800   R/ 400-450
GANSO, EMIL (1895-1941) AMERICAN
I/ 50-300   P/ 150-1000   R/ 330
GANTNER, BERNARD (B. 1930) FRENCH
P/ 100-300
GARBER, DANIEL (1880-1958) AMERICAN
I/ 250-400
GARCIA, HIDALGO JOSE (1656-1712) SPANISH
P/ 400-2200
GARDINER, ELIZA D. (1871-1955) AMERICAN
R/ 100-2400
GARET, JEDD
P/ 300-800
GARNERAY, AMBROSE (1783-1857) FRENCH
I/ 1200
GASSEL, LUCAS (1500-1570) GERMAN
I/ 150-1400
GASSI, FRITZ
P/ 200-600
GAUDY, GEORGES (B. 1872) BELGIAN
P/ 300-4500
GAUG, MARGARET ANN (B. 1909) AMERICAN
I/ 75-200
GAUGENGIGL, IGNAZ MARCEL (1855-1932) AMERICAN
I/ 50-500

GAUGUIN, PAUL (1848-1903) FRENCH
    I/ 175-280544   P/ 700-580000   R/ 200-216000
GAUL, AUGUST (1869-1921) GERMAN
    I/ 250-625   P/ 50-250
GAULTIER, LEONARD (1561-1641) FRENCH
    I/ 200-400
GAUTIER D'AGOTY, JACQUES FABIEN (B. 1710-1781) FRENCH
    I/ 8000-13000
GAVARNI, SULPICE-GUILLAUME C.(called PAUL) (1804-1866) FRENCH
    P/ 30-850
GEARHART, FRANCES (1869-1958) AMERICAN
    R/ 175-1100
GEDNEY, CHARLES (1854-1906) AMERICAN
    I/ 25-100
GEERLINGS, GERALD K. (1889-1958) AMERICAN
    I/ 150-2800
GEIGER, RUPPRECHT (B. 1908) GERMAN
    P/ 50-1200
GEIGER, WILLI (1878-1971) GERMAN
    I/ 40-600   P/ 25-400
GEIS, JOSEPH N.
    P/ 500-2500
GEITLINGER, ERNST
    P/ 250-450
GELLEE, CLAUDE (1600-1682) FRENCH/ITALIAN
    I/ 50-25000
GEN-PAUL (1895-1974) FRENCH
    I/ 100-350   P/ 25-500
GENIN, ROBERT (1884-1934) RUSSIAN
    I/ 50-400   P/ 30-450
GENKINGER, FRITZ (B. 1934) GERMAN
    P/ 100-300
GEORGES, JOANNES (19TH C) FRENCH
    P/ 1000-2500
GERICAULT, JEAN-LOUIS ANDRES THEODORE (1791-1824) FRENCH
    P/ 200-63000
GERITZ, FRANZ (1895-1945) AMERICAN
    R/ 200-400
GERUNG, MATHIAS (1500-1568) GERMAN
    R/ 1100-2100
GERVAIS, PAUL JEAN LOUIS (1859-1936) FRENCH
    P/ 100
GESMAR, CHARLES (?) ?
    P/ 500-4200

Technique Key

Under each <u>printing technique</u> you may encounter the following types of prints (or combination of processes):

- **I** <u>Intaglio:</u>
  - etching
  - drypoint
  - steel engraving
  - stipple engraving
  - aquatint
  - mezzotint
  - soft-ground etching
  - crayon manner

- **P** <u>Planographic:</u>
  - lithograph
  - monotype
  - silk-screen
  - cliche verre
  - serigraph

- **R** <u>Relief:</u>
  - wood block
    - woodcut
      - chiaroscuro
    - wood engraving
  - linoleum cut (linocut)

GESSNER, RICHARD (1894-1989) GERMAN
I/ 200-350
GESSNER, SALOMON (1730-1788) SWISS
I/ 25-550
GESTEL, LEENDERT (1881-1941) DUTCH
P/ 800
GEYER, HAROLD (B. 1905) AMERICAN
I/ 25-100
GEYLING, REMIGIUS
P/ 25-800
GEYSER, CHRISTIAN (1742-1803) GERMAN
I/ 550-650
GHEYN, JACOB DE I (1532-1582) DUTCH
I/ 3200
GHEYN, JACOB DE II (1565-1629) DUTCH
I/ 100-14300
GHEYN, JACOB DE III (1596-1641) DUTCH
I/ 800
GHISI, DIANA (1536-1590) ITALIAN
I/ 5000
GHISI, GIORGIO (1520-1582) ITALIAN
I/ 100-39000
GHISI, GIOVANNI BATTISTA (1498-1563) ITALIAN
I/ 60-3200
GIACOMETTI, ALBERTO (1901-1966) SWISS
I/ 180-14000   P/ 50-10500
GIACOMETTI, AUGUSTO (1877-1947) SWISS
P/ 800-2300
GIACOMETTI, GIOVANNI (1868-1933) ?
P/ 100-3200   R/ 250-6600
GIBRAL, ANTON (?) ?
P/ 500
GIGER, HANS-RUEDI (?) ?
P/ 75-1000
GIKOW, RUTH (1914-1982) AMERICAN
P/ 25-100   R/ 240
GILL, ERIC (1882-1940) BRITISH
R/ 125-1000
GILLES, WERNER (1894-1961) GERMAN
P/ 150-1250   R/ 600
GILLETTA, FRANCOIS (20TH C) FRENCH
I/ 375
GILLOT, CLAUDE (1673-1722) FRENCH
I/ 40-400

GILLRAY, JAMES (1757-1815) BRITISH
I/ 25-1500
GILMOUR, LEON (1907-1989) AMERICAN
R/ 350-550
GIMMI, WILHELM (1886-1960) SWISS
P/ 25-350
GINNER, CHARLES (1878-1952) BRITISH
R/ 400-600
GIORDANO, LUCA (1632-1705) ITALIAN
I/ 100-13000
GIPKENS, JULIUS
P/ 1200-2200
GIRARD, ANDRE (20TH C) FRENCH
P/ 500-2800
GIRARDET, PAUL (1821-1893) FRENCH
I/ 2200
GIRBAL, GASTON (?) ?
P/ 300-1500
GIRKE, RAIMUND (B. 1930) GERMAN
P/ 100-320
GIRTIN, THOMAS (1775-1802) BRITISH
I/ 550
GISCH, WILLIAM (B. 1906) AMERICAN
P/ 75-400
GLACKENS, WILLIAM J. (1870-1938) AMERICAN
P/ 1500-3000
GLARNER, FRITZ (1899-1972) SWISS
P/ 400-5300
GLEIZES, ALBERT (1881-1953) FRENCH
I/ 140-5000   P/ 125-3300
GLINES, DAVID (B. 1931) AMERICAN
I/ 25-100   R/ 25-100
GLOVER, D.L. (?) ?
I/ 1100
GMELIN, WILHELM (1760-1820) GERMAN
I/ 200-450
GNOLI, DOMENICO (1933-1970) ITALIAN
P/ 700-7400
GOENEUTTE, NORBERT (1854-1894) FRENCH
I/ 125-1100   P/ 200
GOERG, EDOUARD (1893-1969) FRENCH
I/ 25-1900   P/ 50-775
GOFF, LLOYD (B. 1917) AMERICAN
P/ 25-100

GOGH, VINCENT VAN (1853-1890) DUTCH
I/ 95000-165500   P/ 165495
GOINES, DAVID LANCE (20TH C) AMERICAN
P/ 150-1980
GOLDTHWAITE, ANNE WILSON (1869-1944) AMERICAN
I/ 40-125
GOLDYNE, JOSEPH (20TH C) AMERICAN
I/ 500   P/ 600-800
GOLE, JACOB (1660-1737) DUTCH
I/ 200-1558
GOLINKIN, JOSEPH WEBSTER (1896-1964) AMERICAN
P/ 100-770
GOLTZIUS, HENDRIK (1558-1616) FLEMISH
I/ 50-32300   R/ 300-96000
GONTCHAROVA, NATALIA (1881-1962) RUSSIAN
P/ 100-6000
GOODE, JOE (B. 1937) AMERICAN
P/ 125-350
GOODMAN, ARTHUR J. (19TH C) BRITISH
P/ 2200
GOODMAN, BERTRAM (B. 1904) AMERICAN
P/ 40-100
GOODNOUGH, ROBERT (B. 1917) AMERICAN
P/ 25-200
GORDON, JEFFREY (?) ?
P/ 20-250
GORGONI, M. (?) ?
P/ 2000
GORIN, JEAN (1899-1981) FRENCH
P/ 90-350
GORKY, ARSHILE (1904-1948) AMERICAN
P/ 3500-28000
GORMAN, R.C. (B. 1933) AMERICAN
P/ 200-1300
GORNIK, APRIL (B. 1953) AMERICAN
I/ 450-1800   R/ 3575
GORSLINE, DOUGLAS (1913-1985) AMERICAN
I/ 300-660
GOSSAERT, JAN (called MABUSE) (15TH/16TH C) FLEMISH
R/ 5000-14000
GOTHEIN, WERNER
R/ 25-2100
GOTSCH, FRIEDRICH (1900-1984) GERMAN
I/ 630-1700   P/ 75-6700   R/ 100-63

GOTTLIEB, ADOLPH (1903-1974) AMERICAN
I/ 800-3900   P/ 200-5000
GOTTLIEB, MAXIM B. (B. 1903) AMERICAN
P/ 25-100
GOTTLOB, FERNAND (B. 1873) FRENCH
P/ 275-1800
GOTTSCHICK, JOHANN CHRISTIAN BENJAMIN (1776-1844) GERMAN
I/ 400-1400
GOTZ, KARL OTTO (B. 1914) GERMAN
P/ 300-5600   R/ 1400
GOUDT, HENDRIK (1585-1648) DUTCH
I/ 40-25000
GOURMONT, JEAN DE I/ (16TH C) FRENCH
I/ 700-6200   R/ 1500
GOUWEN, WILLEM VAN (17TH/18TH C) DUTCH
I/ 250-1600
GOYA Y LUCIENTES, FRANCISCO JOSE DE (1746-1828) SPANISH
I/ 90-129000   P/ 341000
GRAESER, CAMILLE (B. 1892) SWISS
P/ 400-500
GRAF, OSKAR (B. 1870) GERMAN
I/ 200-700
GRAF, URS (1485-1527) SWISS
R/ 100-26000
GRAFF, ANTON (1736-1813) GERMAN
I/ 175-2000
GRAHAM, ROBERT ALEXANDER (1873-1946) AMERICAN
I/ 150-400   P/ 400
GRAMATTE, WALTER (1897-1929) GERMAN
I/ 25-3000   P/ 100-3500   R/ 200-1200
GRANIE (1866-1915) FRENCH
P/ 200
GRANT, GORDON HOPE (1875-1962) AMERICAN
I/ 100-450   P/ 50-400
GRASS, GUNTER (B. 1927) GERMAN
I/ 25-450   P/ 925
GRASSET, EUGENE (1841-1917) FRENCH
I/ 300-400   P/ 70-6000
GRAUMANN, ERWIN (B. 1902) GERMAN
I/ 200-450
GRAVES, MORRIS COLE (B. 1910) AMERICAN
P/ 200
GRAVES, NANCY (B. 1940) AMERICAN
I/ 935   P/ 50-1100

GRAY, HENRY PETERS (1819-1877) AMERICAN
P/ 200-3100
GREAVES, DERRICK (B. 1927) BRITISH
P/ 150
GRECO, EMILIO (B. 1913) ITALIAN
I/ 200-600   P/ 255
GREEN, RUSSELL (1856-1940) AMERICAN
P/ 40-100
GREEN, SAMUEL M. (B. 1909) AMERICAN
I/ 25-100
GREEN, VALENTINE (B. 1739-1813) BRITISH
I/ 450-4300
GREENWOOD, JOHN (1727-1792) AMERICAN
I/ 250-625
GREINER, OTTO (1869-1916) GERMAN
I/ 275-1300   P/ 200-950
GRENIER, FRANCOIS (?) ?
P/ 125-525
GRIEN, HANS BALDUNG (1484-1545) GERMAN
R/ 150-26000
GRIESHABER, HAP (B. 1909) GERMAN
P/ 50-12600   R/ 25-20000
GRIGGS, FREDERICK L. (1876-1938) BRITISH
I/ 125-2900
GRIGNON, P. F.
P/ 300-400
GRIMALDI, GIOVANNI FRANCESCO (1606-1680) ITALIAN
I/ 100-925
GRIMM, LUDWIG EMIL (1790-1863) GERMAN
I/ 100-1600
GRIMM, WILLEM
I/ 150-400   P/ 50-325   R/ 100-350
GRIS, JUAN (1887-1927) SPANISH
P/ 125-5000
GROMAIRE, MARCEL (1892-1971) FRENCH
I/ 35-1650
GRONOWSKI, TADEUSZ
P/ 1000-1700
GROOMS, RED (B. 1937) AMERICAN
I/ 100-3300   P/ 175-17600   R/ 6600
GROPPER, WILLIAM (1897-1977) AMERICAN
I/ 150-350   P/ 25-1100
GROS, ANTOINE JEAN BARON (1771-1835) FRENCH
P/ 1400-2300

GROSS, CHAIM (1904-1991) AMERICAN
P/ 25-660
GROSS, HANS (?) GERMAN
R/ 150-450
GROSSMAN, EDWIN BOOTH (1887-19570 AMERICAN
P/ 75-175
GROSSMANN, RUDOLF (1882-1941) GERMAN
I/ 80-1400   P/ 25-1035
GROSZ, GEORGE (1893-1959) AMERICAN
I/ 200-1600   P/ 24-5400
GROTH, JOHN (B. 1908) AMERICAN
I/ 25-100
GRUAU, RENE
P/ 800-1500
GRUBER, HEINRICH R. (15TH C) GERMAN
I/ 25   P/ 50
GRUN, JULES ALEXANDRE (1868-1934) FRENCH
P/ 150-5100
GRUTZKE, JOHANNES (B. 1937)
I/ 125-300   P/ 170-325
GUBITZ, FRIEDRICH (1786-1870) GERMAN
R/ 400-700
GUDIN, ROBERT
P/ 2200
GUERCINO, (GIOVANNI F. IL BARBIERI) (1591-1666) ITALIAN
I/ 200-300
GUERIN, CHARLES (1875-1939) FRENCH
P/ 40-1000
GUIDO, RAFFAELO
I/ 150-700
GUILBEAU, HONORE (B. 1907) AMERICAN
P/ 20-100
GUILLAME, ALBERT (1873-1942) FRENCH
P/ 200-3100
GULBRANSSON, OLAF (B. 1873) NORWEGIAN
P/ 75-1000
GULDENMUNDT, HANS (D. 1560) GERMAN
R/ 15400
GUNST, PIETER STEVENS VAN (1659-1724) DUTCH
I/ 50-125
GURR, LENA (B. 1897) AMERICAN
P/ 100-350

Technique Key

Under each <u>printing technique</u> you may encounter the following types of prints (or combination of processes):

- **I** <u>Intaglio:</u>
  - etching
  - drypoint
  - steel engraving
  - stipple engraving
  - aquatint
  - mezzotint
  - soft-ground etching
  - crayon manner

- **P** <u>Planographic:</u>
  - lithograph
  - monotype
  - silk-screen
  - cliche verre
  - serigraph

- **R** <u>Relief:</u>
  - wood block
    - woodcut
      - chiaroscuro
    - wood engraving
  - linoleum cut (linocut)

GUSTON, PHILIP (1912-1980) AMERICAN
  P/ 200-5500
GUTTUSO, RENATO (B. 1912) ITALIAN
  I/ 150-900   P/ 125-1300
GWATHMEY, ROBERT (1903-1989) AMERICAN
  P/ 200-1600
GYARMATY, MICHEL (?) ?
  P/ 3000-5000

H

HAAGENSEN, F. (19TH C) EUROPEAN
  I/ 25-75
HAAS, RICHARD (B. 1936) AMERICAN
  I/ 200-1500   P/ 350
HACKAERT, JAN (1629-1699) DUTCH
  I/ 700
HACKERT, JACOB PHILIPPE (1737-1807) GERMAN
  I/ 75
HADEN, FRANCIS SEYMOUR (1818-1910) BRITISH
  I/ 50-6900
HAGERMAN, KURT (20TH C) AMERICAN
  I/ 25-100
HAGHE, LOUIS (1806-1885) BELGIAN
  P/ 50
HAGIWARA, HIDEO (B. 1913) JAPANESE
  R/ 25-1650
HAID, JOHANN ELIAS (1780-1809) GERMAN
  I/ 175-4700
HAID, JOHANN JAKOB (1704-1767) GERMAN
  I/ 100-550
HAID, JOHANN LORENZ (1702-1750) GERMAN
  I/ 200-350
HAIG, AXEL H. (1835-1921) SWEDISH
  I/ 50-200
HAJDU, ETIENNE (B. 1907) FRENCH
  I/ 250-3200
HAJEK, OTTO H. (B. 1927) GERMAN
  P/ 25-500
HALL, ARTHUR W. (1889-1981) AMERICAN

I/ 25-100
HALL, OLIVER (1869-1957) BRITISH
  I/ 25-75
HALLIDAY, C. J. (2OTH C) AMERICAN
  R/ 25-75
HALM, PETER (B. 1854) GERMAN
  I/ 75-500
HALTEN, E. (?) ?
  I/ 275
HAM, GEORGES
  P/ 150-10450
HAMAGUCHI, YOZO (B. 1909) JAPANESE
  I/ 400-57750   P/ 900-2100
HAMILTON, HAMILTON (1847-1928) AMERICAN
  I/ 50-650
HAMILTON, RICHARD (B. 1922) BRITISH
  I/ 35-26100   P/ 175-11000
HANKEY, WILLIAM LEE (1869-1952) BRITISH
  I/ 30-500
HANNA, BOYD (B. 1907) AMERICAN
  I/ 25-100
HANSEN, ARMIN CARL (1886-1957) AMERICAN
  I/ 200-4700
HANSEN, DIANA (20TH C) AMERICAN
  P/ 50-200
HANSEN-BAHIA, K.H.
  R/ 25-1500
HANSI (1873-1951) FRENCH
  P/ 200-275
HARDY, DUDLEY (1865-1922) BRITISH
  P/ 200-4000
HARING, KEITH (1958-1990) AMERICAN
  I/ 350   P/ 400-27600
HARNEST, FRITZ (B. 1905) GERMAN
  R/ 200-900
HARPIGNIES, HENRI JOSEPH (1819-1916) FRENCH
  I/ 1200
HARRIS, SAM HYDE (20TH C) AMERICAN
  R/ 100-715
HARRY, PHILIP (active 1833-1857) CANADIAN
  P/ 250-750
HART, GEORGE O. ("POP") (1868-1933) AMERICAN
  I/ 50-400   P/ 175-350
HARTLEY, MARSDEN (1878-1943) AMERICAN

P/ 175-4400
HARTMAN, BERTRAM (1882-1960) AMERICAN
P/ 30-100
HARTMANN, HANS (B. 1845) GERMAN
P/ 900
HARTRICK, ARCHIBALD STANDISH (1864-1950) BRITISH
P/ 50-200
HARTUNG, HANS (1904-1989) GERMAN
    I/ 200-8100   P/ 100-3100   R/ 300-1600
HASEGAWA, KIYOSHI (B. 1891) JAPANESE
    I/ 800-57400   P/ 1000-4200   R/ 900-47000
HASEGAWA, SHOICHI (B. 1929) JAPANESE
    I/ 60-780   P/ 250
HASKELL, ERNEST (1876-1925) AMERICAN
    I/ 25-300   P/ 660
HASSALL, JOHN (1868-1948) BRITISH
P/ 800-1900
HASSAM, FREDERICK CHILDE (1859-1935) AMERICAN
    I/ 200-25300   P/ 400-6050
HASUI, KAWASE (1883-1957) JAPANESE
    R/ 150-6600
HAUPTMANN, IVO (B. 1886) BRITISH
    I/ 175-500   P/ 175-250
HAUSER, ERICH (B. 1930) GERMAN
    I/ 150-400   P/ 440
HAUSNER, RUDOLF (B. 1914) AUSTRIAN
    I/ 25-200   P/ 125-550
HAUSSMANN, RAOUL (1886-1971) AUSTRIAN
    R/ 125-1600
HAVELL, WILLIAM (1782-1857) BRITISH
P/ 700-1000
HAYTER, STANLEY WILLIAM (1901-1988) BRITISH/AMERICAN
    I/ 50-8800   P/ 50-825
HEARTFIELD, JOHN (1891-1968) GERMAN
P/ 600
HEASLIP, WILLIAM (1898-1970) AMERICAN
    I/ 50-125
HEBERT, MARIAN (1899-1960) AMERICAN
    I/ 25-350
HECHT, JOSEPH (1891-1951) POLISH/BRITISH
    I/ 75-200
HECKE, JAN VAN DEN (1620-1684) DUTCH
    I/ 50-600
HECKEL, ERICH (1883-1970) GERMAN

I/ 50-20000   P/ 100-39000   R/ 25-385000
HEEMSKERCK, JACOB EDUARD VAN BEEST (1828-1894) DUTCH
    R/ 100-950
HEEMSKERCK, MAERTEN (1498-1578) DUTCH
    I/ 30-1700
HEGENBARTH, JOSEF (1884-1962) GERMAN
    I/ 40-575   P/ 150-350
HEILIGER, BERNHARD (B. 1915) GERMAN
    I/ 200-525   P/ 50-850
HEINE, THOMAS TH. (B. 1867) GERMAN
    I/ 100-450   P/ 50-2900   R/ 1200
HEINTZELMAN, ARTHUR W. (1891-1965) AMERICAN
    I/ 40-200
HEISE, WILHELM (B. 1892) GERMAN
    P/ 300-450
HEIZER, MICHAEL (B. 1944) AMERICAN
    I/ 900-2000
HELBIG, WALTER (B. 1878) GERMAN
    R/ 25-650
HELDT, WERNER (1904-1954) GERMAN
    P/ 150-2000   R/ 1585
HELFOND, RIVA (B. 1910) AMERICAN
    P/ 25-300
HELLEU, PAUL CESAR (1859-1927) FRENCH
    I/ 50-15600   P/ 100-1500
HELMAN, ISIDORE S. (1743-1809) FRENCH
    I/ 200
HEMELMAN, ALBERT
    P/ 800-1700
HENRION, ARMAND FRANCOIS JOSEPH (B. 1875) FRENCH
    I/ 120-200   P/ 550
HERBIG, OTTO (1889-1971) GERMAN
    P/ 100-900
HERBIN, AUGUSTE (1882-1960) FRENCH
    P/ 100-5700
HERKENRATH, PETER (B. 1900) GERMAN
    R/ 275
HERKOMER, HUBERT VON (1849-1914) BRITISH
    I/ 100-400
HERMES, ERICH (B. 1881) GERMAN
    P/ 800
HERMES, GERTRUDE (1901-1983) BRITISH
    R/ 500
HERMS, GEORGE (20TH C) AMERICAN

P/ 100-200
HERRMANN, PAUL (B. 1864) GERMAN
   I/ 100-300   P/ 150-600
HESSE, EVA (1936-1970) AMERICAN
   P/ 1800
HEUBNER, FRITZ
   I/ 25-60
HEYBOER, ANTON (B. 1924) DUTCH
   I/ 75-2200
HILAIRE, CAMILLE (B. 1916) FRENCH
   P/ 40-525
HILER, HILAIRE (1898-1966) AMERICAN
   P/ 75-225
HILL, JOHN WILLIAM (1812-1879)(after) AMERICAN
   I/ 770-7150
HILL, POLLY K. (B. 1900) AMERICAN
   I/ 25-100
HILLS, ROBERT (1769-1844) BRITISH
   I/ 150
HIRSCH, JOSEPH (1910-1981) AMERICAN
   P/ 75-1700
HIRSCH, KARL JAKOB (B. 1892) GERMAN
   I/ 150-350
HIRSCHFELD, ALBERT (B. 1903) AMERICAN
   I/ 110   P/ 500-1320
HIRSCHVOGEL, AUGUSTIN (1503-1553) GERMAN
   I/ 200-60000
HJORTZBERG, OLLE (1872-1959) SWEDISH
   P/ 1200-2900
HOBBS, MORRIS HENRY (B. 1892) AMERICAN
   I/ 40-150
HOCKELMANN, ANTONIUS (B. 1937) ?
   I/ 125-525   P/ 331   R/ 200-700
HOCKNEY, DAVID (B. 1937) BRITISH
   I/ 100-49500   P/ 75-316800
HODGKIN, HOWARD (B. 1932) BRITISH
   I/ 400-13240   P/ 200-29700
HODLER, FERDINAND (1853-1918) SWISS
   I/ 300   P/ 100-3700   R/ 1700
HOEHME, GERHARD (B. 1920) GERMAN
   I/ 400-5600   P/ 850-1600
HOESEN, BETH VAN
   I/ 150-1500
HOFBAUER, ARNOST (B. 1869)

P/ 1100-1750
HOFER, KARL (1878-1955) GERMAN
    I/ 100-6200   P/ 40-2100   R/ 630-940
HOFFMAN, GUSTAVE (1869-1945) AMERICAN
    I/ 25-100
HOFKUNST, ALFRED (B. 1942) SWISS
    I/ 275-1000
HOFFMAN, IRWIN D. (1901-1989) AMERICAN
    I/ 40-300
HOFMANN, HANS (1880-1966) AMERICAN
    P/ 200-3300
HOFMANN, LUDWIG (1832-1895) GERMAN
    I/ 100-250   P/ 25-250   R/ 50-740
HOGARTH, WILLIAM (1697-1764) BRITISH
    I/ 25-4000
HOGUE, ALEXANDER (B. 1898) AMERICAN
    P/ 200-400
HOHENSTEIN, ADOLF (1854-1917) GERMAN
    P/ 600-5500
HOHLWEIN, LUDWIG (?) ?
    I/ 110   P/ 175-11000   R/ 500
HOLLAND, TOM (B. 1936) AMERICAN
    I/ 400-1100   P/ 100-500
HOLLAR, WENCESLAUS (1607-1677) BOHEMIAN
    I/ 25-12000
HOLLENBERG, FELIX (1868-1945) GERMAN
    I/ 100-400
HOLST, ROLAND (B. 1869) DUTCH
    P/ 200-600
HOLTZ, KARL (B. 1899) GERMAN
    I/ 400   P/ 300-1600   R/ 300
HOLZER, JOHANN E. (B. 1875) GERMAN
    I/ 400-1200
HOMER, WINSLOW (1836-1910) AMERICAN
    I/ 50-31000   P/ 43000-68750
HONDIUS, HENDRIK (17TH C) DUTCH
    I/ 200-1000
HOOD, THOMAS R. (B. 1910) AMERICAN
    I/ 25-100
HOOK, SANDY
    P/ 275-2100
HOOVER, ELLISON (1888-1955) AMERICAN
    P/ 100-200
HOPFER, DANIEL (1470-1536) DUTCH

Technique Key

Under each <u>printing technique</u> you may encounter the following types of prints (or combination of processes):

- **I** <u>Intaglio:</u>
  - etching
  - drypoint
  - steel engraving
  - stipple engraving
  - aquatint
  - mezzotint
  - soft-ground etching
  - crayon manner

- **P** <u>Planographic:</u>
  - lithograph
  - monotype
  - silk-screen
  - cliche verre
  - serigraph

- **R** <u>Relief:</u>
  - wood block
    - woodcut
      - chiaroscuro
    - wood engraving
  - linoleum cut (linocut)

I/ 50-24000
HOPFER, HIERONYMUS (1525-1550) DUTCH
I/ 30-1675
HOPFER, LAMBERT (16TH C) DUTCH
I/ 75-6600
HOPFNER, WILHELM
I/ 300-600
HOPKINS, EDNA BOIES (1872-1937) AMERICAN
R/ 1500-3100
HOPPER, EDWARD (1882-1967) AMERICAN
I/ 800-52250
HOPPNER, JOHN (1758-1810) BRITISH
I/ 350
HORNBY, LESTER GEORGE (1882-1956) AMERICAN
I/ 25-400
HORTER, EARL (1881-1940) AMERICAN
I/ 40-275
HOSFORD, HARRY L. (1877-1945) AMERICAN
I/ 25-100
HOWE, R.C. (19TH/20TH C) AMERICAN
R/ 100-200
HOYLAND, JOHN (B. 1934) BRITISH
I/ 332   P/ 200-800
HOYTON, EDWARD BOUVERIE (1900-1988) BRITISH
I/ 50-250
HRDLICKA, ALFRED (B. 1928) AUSTRIAN
I/ 25-2000   P/ 50-1200
HUBBUCH, KARL (B. 1891)
I/ 125-3200   P/ 200-6500   R/ 150-1200
HUBER, ERNST (1896-1960) AUSTRIAN
P/ 15-60
HUCHTENBURG, JAN VAN (1646-1733) DUTCH
I/ 50-1300
HUET, PAUL (1803-1869) FRENCH
I/ 200-700
HUGIN, KARL (B. 1887) SWISS
I/ 100-450
HUNDERTWASSER, FRIEDRICH (B. 1928) AUSTRIAN
I/ 330-4700   P/ 85-10500   R/ 800-5800
HUNT, BRYAN (B. 1947) AMERICAN
I/ 3000-5500   R/ 605
HUNT, LEIGH (1858-1937) AMERICAN
I/ 30-75
HUNT, WILLIAM HENRY (1790-1864) BRITISH

I/ 75-1100   P/ 660
HUNTER, COLIN (1841-1904) BRITISH
  I/ 30-100
HUNTER, MEL (B. 1927) AMERICAN
  P/ 25
HUNTLEY, VICTORIA HUTSON (1900-1971) AMERICAN
  P/ 40-450
HUNZIKER, MAX
  I/ 25-2100   P/ 100-300
HURD, PETER (1904-1984) AMERICAN
  P/ 250-1210
HURLEY, EDWARD TIMOTHY (1869-1950) AMERICAN
  I/ 75-200
HUSZAR, VILMOS (B. 1884) DUTCH
  I/ 800   R/ 1500-2400
HUTTER, WOLFGANG (B. 1928) AUSTRIAN
  I/ 40-200
HUYBRECHTS, ADRIAEN (active 1573-1614) GERMAN ?
  I/ 400-750
HYDE, HELEN H. (1868-1919) AMERICAN
  I/ 100-400   R/ 50-1800
HYMAN, MOSES (B. 1870) AMERICAN
  I/ 25-100
HYNCHES, RAOUL (B. 1893) DUTCH
  P/ 300-1500

I

IBELS, HENRI GABRIELLE (1867-1936) FRENCH
  I/ 660   P/ 50-4000
ICART, LOUIS (1888-1950) FRENCH
  I/ 400-30000   P/ 200-5500
IHLE, JOHN (B. 1925) AMERICAN
  I/ 20-75
ILLIES, ARTHUR (B. 1870) GERMAN
  I/ 75-850   P/ 200-800   R/ 250-315
IMMENDORFF, JORG (B. 1945) GERMAN
  P/ 300-1300   R/ 150-10500
IMPERIALE, GIROLAMO (D. 1630) ITALIAN
  I/ 700-1400

INDIANA, ROBERT (B. 1928) AMERICAN
   P/ 50-6000
INGRAHAM, KATHERINE (1900-1982) AMERICAN
   I/ 25-100
INGRES, JEAN AUGUSTE DOMINIQUE (1780-1867) FRENCH
   I/ 275-2000   P/ 1900-11000
INMAN, PAULINE W. (B. 1904) AMERICAN
   R/ 25-100
IONESCO, EUGENE (B. 1912) FRENCH
   P/ 200-275
ISABEY, JEAN BAPTISTE (1767-1855) FRENCH
   P/ 40-100
ISABEY, EUGENE (1803-1886) FRENCH
   P/ 200-400
ISELI, ROLF (B. 1934) SWISS
   I/ 175-1600   P/ 100-1500
ISRAELS, JOSEF (1824-1911) DUTCH
   I/ 100-700
ITTEN, JOHANNES (1888-1967) SWISS/GERMAN
   P/ 220-3100
ITURRINO, FRANCESCO (1864-1924) SPANISH
   I/ 300

J

JACKSON, F. ERNEST (20TH C) AMERICAN
   P/ 100-300
JACKSON, JOHN B. (1778-1831) BRITISH
   R/ 88-3540
JACOB, WALTER (B. 1893) GERMAN
   P/ 250   R/ 200-3000
JACOBSEN, ROBERT (B. 1912) DANISH
   I/ 393-600   P/ 200-650
JACOBY, JOHANN (1733-1797) GERMAN
   P/ 900-1000
JACOULET, PAUL (1902-1960) FRENCH
   P/ 275   R/ 130-25000
JACQUE, CHARLES EMILE (1813-1894) FRENCH
   I/ 25-7000
JACQUEMIN, ANDRE (B. 1904) FRENCH

I/ 75-600
JACQUES, BERTHA CLAUSEN (1863-1941) AMERICAN
I/ 50-100
JACQUETTE, YVONNE (B. 1934) AMERICAN
   I/ 1200   P/ 2000-3100   R/ 4620
JAECKEL, WILLI (1888-1944) GERMAN
   I/ 50-750   P/ 75-4700   R/ 250
JAHN, GEORG (B. 1869) GERMAN
   P/ 400
JAMNITZER, C.
   I/ 200-550
JANINET, JEAN F. (1752-1814) FRENCH
   I/ 150-16000
JANSEN, FRNZ MARIA (1885-1958) GERMAN
   I/ 125-828   R/ 25-2200
JANSSEN, HORST (1929-1990) DUTCH
   I/ 20-5300   P/ 75-7300   R/ 1000-25800
JAWLENSKY, ALEXEI VON (1864-1941) GERMAN
   P/ 300-20600
JEANNIOT, GEORGES (1848-1934) FRENCH
   I/ 25-400
JEGHER, CHRISTOFFEL (1596-1653) GERMAN
   R/ 350-31500
JENICHEN, BALTHASAR (D. 1621)
   I/ 300
JENKINS, PAUL (B. 1923) AMERICAN
   P/ 50-2100
JENSEN, ALFRED J. (1903-1981) AMERICAN
   P/ 300-1400
JETTMAR, RUDOLF (B. 1869) POLISH
   I/ 200-400
JIRLOW, LENNART (20TH C) GERMAN
   P/ 500-2200
JOBBE-DUVAL, GASTON (20TH C) FRENCH
   P/ 250-700
JODE, PIETER DE II (1606-1674)
   I/ 25-375
JOHN, AUGUSTUS (1878-1961) BRITISH
   I/ 100-1700   P/ 75-600
JOHNS, JASPER (B. 1930) AMERICAN
   I/ 150-58000   P/ 270-500000
JOHNSON, AVERY F. (B. 1906) AMERICAN
   I/ 25-100
JOHNSON, WILLIAM (20TH C) AMERICAN

P/ 1600-2000
JONES, ALLEN (B. 1937) BRITISH
　　P/ 50-4900
JONES, DAVID (1895-1974) BRITISH
　　I/ 50-125
JONES, JOE (OR JOSEPH JOHN) (1909-1963) AMERICAN
　　I/ 1640　　P/ 500
JONGKIND, JOHAN BARTHOLD (1819-1891) DUTCH
　　I/ 100-8300
JORN, ASGER (1914-1973) DANISH
　　I/ 75-4600　　P/ 88-9800　　R/ 1400-5000
JOSSOT, HENRI GUSTAVE (B. 1866) FRENCH
　　P/ 400-650
JOUVE, PAUL (1880-1973) FRENCH
　　I/ 125-2200　　P/ 608　　R/ 90-150
JOYAU, AMEDEE (B. 1872) FRENCH
　　R/ 150
JUDD, DONALD (B. 1928) AMERICAN
　　I/ 275-3000　　P/ 400-1500　　R/ 275-6000
JULES, MERVIN (B. 1912) AMERICAN
　　P/ 40-160
JUNGNICKEL, LUDWIG HEINRICH (1881-1965) GERMAN
　　I/ 150-260　　P/ 25-450　　R/ 200-3200
JUSTE, JUSTE DE (1505-1559) FRENCH
　　I/ 500-26000

K

KAGY, SHEFFIELD (B. 1907) AMERICAN
　　R/ 50-150
KALAS, ERNEST (B. 1861) FRENCH
　　P/ 2400-3500
KALCKREUTH, KARL WALTER LEOPOLD VON (1855-1925) GERMAN
　　I/ 50-650
KALER, JOHANN (?) ?
　　I/ 30-100
KALIONWSKI, HORST EGON (B. 1924) GERMAN
　　I/ 100-450　　P/ 200-400
KALLMORGEN, FRIEDRICH (1856-1924) GERMAN
　　P/ 125-425

KAMMULLER, PAUL (B. 1885) GERMAN
P/ 600-1100
KAMPMANN, GUSTAV (1859-1917) GERMAN
P/ 100-400
KANDINSKY, WASSILY (1866-1944) RUSSIAN
I/ 500-15900   P/ 250-175000   R/ 22-110000
KANEIAN, A. (20TH C) AMERICAN
P/ 75-150
KANOLDT, ALEXANDER (1881-1939) GERMAN
P/ 100-3800
KAPLAN, ANATOLI (B. 1903) RUSSIAN
P/ 150-760
KAPPEL, PHILIP (1901-1981) AMERICAN
I/ 50-250
KARDON, DENNIS (?) ?
R/ 100-225
KARSCH, JOACHIM (B. 1897) GERMAN
I/ 350-1900
KASIMIR, LUIGI (1881-1956) AUSTRIAN
I/ 50-1100   P/ 25-175   R/ 300
KASIMIR-HOERNES, T. (FANNA) (B. 1887) AUSTRIAN
I/ 200-375   P/ 25
KATELHON, HERMANN (?) ?
I/ 100-1400   P/ 100-325
KATZ, ALEX (B. 1927) AMERICAN
I/ 450-21100   P/ 100-27000   R/ 300-5000
KATZ, HILDA (B. 1909) AMERICAN
R/ 25-100
KATZIEFF, JULIUS (1892-1957) AMERICAN
P/ 40-150
KAUFFER, E. MCKNIGHT (?) ?
P/ 150-11000
KAUFFMAN, ANGELICA (1740-1807) SWISS
I/ 275-1300
KAUFFMAN, CRAIG (B. 1932) AMERICAN
P/ 400-475
KAUL, AUGUST (B. 1873) GERMAN
I/ 175
KAUS, MAX (1891-1977) GERMAN
I/ 175-1500   P/ 25-8900   R/ 50-3000
KECK, LEO (?) ?
P/ 1100
KEIMEL, HERMANN (B. 1889) GERMAN
P/ 3100

Technique Key

Under each printing technique you may encounter the following types of prints (or combination of processes):

- **I** Intaglio:
  - etching
  - drypoint
  - steel engraving
  - stipple engraving
  - aquatint
  - mezzotint
  - soft-ground etching
  - crayon manner

- **P** Planographic:
  - lithograph
  - monotype
  - silk-screen
  - cliche verre
  - serigraph

- **R** Relief:
  - wood block
    - woodcut
      - chiaroscuro
    - wood engraving
  - linoleum cut (linocut)

KEITH, ELIZABETH (1887-1956) BRITISH
    I/ 100-400   R/ 75-1800
KELLER, HENRY G. (1869-1949) AMERICAN
    I/ 30-220   P/ 75-150
KELLER, LAURENT F. (B. 1855) FRENCH
    P/ 2100
KELLOGG, HAROLD F. (B. 1887) AMERICAN
    I/ 25-100
KELLY, ELLSWORTH (B. 1923) AMERICAN
    I/ 500-6100   P/ 100-34100
KENT, ROCKWELL (1882-1971) AMERICAN
    I/ 20   P/ 50-2800   R/ 50-3300
KERKOVIUS, IDA (1879-1970) GERMAN
    P/ 175-1100
KERSCHBAUMER, ANTON (B. 1885) GERMAN
    P/ 125-1600   R/ 400
KESSEL, THEODOR VAN (B. 1620) DUTCH
    I/ 300-400
KHNOPFF, FERNAND (1858-1921) BELGIAN
    I/ 400-2000   P/ 150-1000
KHODOSSIEVITCH, N. (?) ?
    P/ 100-650
KIFFER, CHARLES (B. 1902) FRENCH
    P/ 150-3700
KIKOINE, MICHEL (1892-1968) FRENCH
    P/ 325
KILIAN, LUKAS (1579-1637) GERMAN
    I/ 150-735
KINGMAN, EUGENE (B. 1909-1975) AMERICAN
    P/ 25-100
KIRCHNER, ERNST LUDWIG (1880-1938) GERMAN
    I/ 165-94000   P/ 125-680000   R/ 25-142500
KIRMSE, MARGUERITE (1885-1954) AMERICAN
    I/ 40-175
KIRKPATRIACK, DONALD M. (B. 1887) AMERICAN
    I/ 25-100
KIRKEBY, PER (B. 1938) DANISH
    I/ 150-900   P/ 125-1300   R/ 400-700
KISLING, MOISE (1891-1953) POLISH/FRENCH
    I/ 200-3100   P/ 150-2000   R/ 800-1000
KISSEL, IRENE (B. 1904) AMERICAN
    I/ 50-150
KITTENSTEYN, CORNELIS VAN (B. 1600) DUTCH
    I/ 500-1300

KITAJ, RONALD B. (B. 1932) BRITISH/AMERICAN
I/ 75-725   P/ 30-2000
KLAPHECK, KONRAD (B. 1935) GERMAN
I/ 100-1100   P/ 150-1900
KLAUKE, JURGEN (B. 1943) GERMAN
I/ 350-450
KLEE, PAUL (1879-1940) SWISS
I/ 1800-115600   P/ 100-96600
KLEBE, CHARLES E. (20TH C) AMERICAN
R/ 40-75
KLEIBER, HANS (1887-1967) AMERICAN
I/ 40-220
KLEIN, JOHANN ADAM (1792-1875) GERMAN
I/ 75-3100   P/ 1245
KLEINSCHMIDT, PAUL (1883-1949) GERMAN
I/ 50-2200   P/ 200-1400
KLEMM, WALTER (1863-1957) GERMAN
I/ 25-350   P/ 25-800   R/ 50-650
KLENGEL, JOHANN CHRISTIAN (1751-1824) GERMAN
I/ 125-400
KLEUKENS, FRIEDRICH WILHELM (B. 1878) GERMAN
I/ 300   P/ 145-2000
KLIEMANN, CARL H. (B. 1924) GERMAN
I/ 250-550   R/ 50-625
KLINE, FRANZ J. (1910-1962) AMERICAN
R/ 200-2600
KLINGER, JULIUS (B. 1876) AUSTRIAN
P/ 300-1650
KLINGER, MAX (1857-1920) GERMAN
I/ 25-29000   P/ 545
KLOSS, GENE (B. 1903) AMERICAN
I/ 100-1500
KLUZIS, GUSTAV (?) ?
P/ 1400-7000
KNAB, ALBERT (B. 1870) GERMAN
P/ 400-2000
KNAPP, JOSEPH D. (B. 1875) AMERICAN
I/ 15-75
KNIE, FOLF JUN (?) ?
P/ 300-2800
KNIGHT, DAME LAURA (1877-1970) BRITISH
I/ 75-1700   P/ 150-1500
KNIGHT, LOXTON (20TH C) BRITISH
R/ 300

KOBELL, FERDINAND (1740-1799) GERMAN
I/ 60-300
KOBELL, WILHELM VON (1766-1855) GERMAN
I/ 30-5000
KOCH, JOSEF ANTON (1768-1839) GERMAN
I/ 100-3300
KOCH, WALTER (1875-1915) GERMAN
P/ 700-2400
KOGAN, MOISHE (MOISSEJ) (B. 1879) RUSSIAN
R/ 150-1100
KOHN, MISCH (B. 1916) AMERICAN
I/ 350
KOKOSCHKA, OSKAR (1886-1980) AUSTRIAN
I/ 100-2200   P/ 25-32000   R/ 350
KOLAR, JIRI (B. 1914) CZECHOSLOVAKIAN
I/ 100-440   P/ 75-650
KOLB, ALOIS (B. 1875) AUSTRIAN
I/ 15-1200   P/ 169
KOLBE, CARL WILHELM (1757-1835) GERMAN
I/ 75-4700
KOLBE, GEORG (1877-1947) GERMAN
I/ 125-1600   P/ 400-650
KOLLWITZ, KATHE (1867-1945) GERMAN
I/ 100-57000   P/ 70-119000   R/ 500-16000
KONIG, FRIEDRICH (1857-1914) AUSTRIAN
P/ 2600   R/ 456
KONINCK, SALOMON (1609-1656) DUTCH
I/ 200-2800
KOONING, WILLEM DE (B. 1904) DUTCH/AMERICAN
I/ 3300-6600   P/ 135-22000
KOPP, MAX (?) ?
P/ 2000
KOPPEL, HENNING (?) ?
P/ 2600
KORAB, KARL (B. 1937) AMERICAN
I/ 15-1700   P/ 15-650
KOW, ALEXIS (?) ?
P/ 440-2200
KRAEMER, DIETER (B. 1937) GERMAN
I/ 150
KRAMER, JACOB (1892-1962) BRITISH
P/ 250-2400
KRAUS, GUSTAV (1804-1852) GERMAN
P/ 630-1600

KRENEK, CARL (B. 1880) AUSTRIAN
P/ 500-1300　　R/ 150-700
KRESSEL, DIETER (?) ?
I/ 100-1200
KRETSCHMAN, A. (?) ?
P/ 1600
KRETSCHMAR, B. (?) ?
I/ 150-30000　　P/ 100-1100　　R/ 1490
KROLL, LEON (1884-1974) AMERICAN
P/ 150-880
KRONBERG, LOUIS (1872-1964) AMERICAN
I/ 50-150
KROTOWSKI, STEPHAN (?) ?
P/ 2000-4000
KRUCK, CHRISTIAN (?) ?
I/ 100-250　　P/ 75-800
KRUG, LUDWIG (B. 1489-1532) GERMAN
I/ 500-6000　　R/ 275-600
KRUGER, FRANZ (1799-1857) GERMAN
P/ 150-1800
KRUSE, ALEXANDER ZEROIN (B.1890) AMERICAN
P/ 25-100
KUBIN, ALFRED (1877-1959) AUSTRIAN
I/ 80-175　　P/ 25-1200
KUBINYI, KALMIN (1906-1973) AMERICAN
I/ 50-180　　P/ 40-75
KUCHENMEISTER, RAINER (B. 1926) GERMAN
P/ 100-550
KUGLER, RUDOLF (?) ?
I/ 175
KUHLER, OTTO (1894-1977) AMERICAN
I/ 150-850
KUHN, WALT (1877-1949) AMERICAN
I/ 275-525　　P/ 200-1700
KUHNERT, WILHELM FRIEDRICH KARL (1865-1926) GERMAN
I/ 150-1400
KUMM, MARGUERITE E. (B. 1902) AMERICAN
R/ 25-100
KUNIYOSHI, YASUO (1893-1953) AMERICAN
I/ 400-600　　P/ 400-37800
KUNTZ, CARL (1770-1830) GERMAN
P/ 800
KUNZIE, DORIS (B. 1910) AMERICAN
P/ 25-100

KUPFERSCHMID, HERMAN (B. 1885) GERMAN
  I/ 100-300
KUPKA, FRANTISEK (1871-1957) CZECHOSLOVAKIAN
  I/ 300-22000   P/ 400-950   R/ 100-1100
KURTZ, HELMUTH (?) ?
  P/ 800-1200
KURZWEIL, MAXMILIAN (1867-1916) AUSTRIAN
  P/ 175-43000   R/ 85-2800
KUSHNER, ROBERT (B. 1949) AMERICAN
  I/ 1500-2100   P/ 275-8800   R/ 990

L

LAAGE, WILHELM (B. 1868) GERMAN
  R/ 75-2200
LABISSE, FELIX (B. 1905) FRENCH
  P/ 45-1100
LABORDE, CHARLES (1886-1941) FRENCH
  R/ 25-200
LABOUREUR, JEAN-EMILE (1877-1943) FRENCH
  I/ 40-11000   P/ 100-4900   R/ 75-5900
LACHNIT, WILHELM (B. 1899) GERMAN
  I/ 375-750   P/ 800
LADANYI, EMORY (B. 1902) AMERICAN
  R/ 25-50
LADENSPELTER, JOHANN (1512-1561) DUTCH
  I/ 200-3800
LAHEY, RICHARD F. (B. 1893) AMERICAN
  I/ 25-100
LAHS, CURT (?) ?
  I/ 250-300   P/ 15-600
LAIRESSE, GERARD DE (1641-1711) FLEMISH
  I/ 75-600
LALANNE, MAXIME (1827-1886) FRENCH
  I/ 40-450
LALLEMAND, GEORGES (1575-1635) FRENCH
  I/ 200-600
LAM, WIFREDO (1902-1982) CUBAN
  I/ 75-2500   P/ 75-1700
LAMBERT, ALFRED (?) ?

P/ 3100
LAMBERT, M.DE (B. 1873) FRENCH
P/ 600
LAMOTTE, BERNARD (B.1903) FRENCH
I/ 30-150
LANA, LODOVICO (1597-1646) ITALIAN
I/ 250-1000
LANDACRE, PAUL H. (1893-1963) AMERICAN
R/ 150-1900
LANDECK, ARMIN (1905-1984) AMERICAN
I/ 150-3500   P/ 200-700
LANDSHUT, MAIR VON (16TH C) GERMAN
I/ 79000
LANE, FITZ HUGH (1804-1865) AMERICAN
P/ 3000-12000
LANE, LOIS (B. 1948) AMERICAN
I/ 225-950
LANE, MIHARU (20TH C) AMERICAN
P/ 30-90
LANFAIR, HARRIET KEESE (B. 1900) AMERICAN
P/ 50-150
LANFRANCO, GIOVANNI (1582-1647) ITALIAN
I/ 200-600
LANG, FRITZ (1877-1961) GERMAN
P/ 250-300   R/ 150-250
LANGE, OTTO (1879-1944) GERMAN
I/ 100-2100   P/ 600   R/ 150-7300
LANGMAID, ROWLAND (20TH C) BRITISH
I/ 225-300
LANSKOY, ANDRE (1902-1976) RUSSIAN/FRENCH
P/ 75-4500
LAP, ENGELBERT (20TH C) AUSTRIAN
R/ 50-125
LAPIQUE, CHARLES (B. 1898) FRENCH
I/ 100-260   P/ 100-600   P/ 100
LARDERA, BERTO (B. 1911) FRENCH
P/ 250
LARMESSIN, NICOLAS (?) ?
I/ 250-550
LARSSON, CARL (1853-1919) SWEDISH
I/ 200-2000   P/ 3000
LARTIGUE, JACQUES (B. 1894) FRENCH

Technique Key

Under each printing technique you may encounter the following types of prints (or combination of processes):

- **I** Intaglio:
    - etching
    - drypoint
    - steel engraving
    - stipple engraving
    - aquatint
    - mezzotint
    - soft-ground etching
    - crayon manner

- **P** Planographic:
    - lithograph
    - monotype
    - silk-screen
    - cliche verre
    - serigraph

- **R** Relief:
    - wood block
        - woodcut
            - chiaroscuro
        - wood engraving
    - linoleum cut (linocut)

P/ 1200
LASANSKY, MAURICIO (B. 1914) AMERICAN
I/ 500-7500
LASKE, OSKAR (1841-1911) AUSTRIAN
I/ 100-550   P/ 100-1400
LASKOFF, FRANZ
P/ 700-6600
LASTMAN, PIETER (1583-1633) DUTCH
I/ 600-4900
LATENAY, GASTON DE (1859-1940) FRENCH
I/ 250   P/ 200-700
LAUBER, JOSEPH (B. 1885) AMERICAN
I/ 30-75
LAUBI, HUGO (?) ?
P/ 200-1500
LAUNAY, NICOLAS DE (1739-1792) FRENCH
I/ 125-7300
LAURENCIN, MARIE (1883-1956) FRENCH
I/ 75-16500   P/ 75-26100
LAURENS, HENRI (1885-1954) FRENCH
I/ 300-4100   P/ 775-3200   R/ 25-800
LAURENT, ERNEST-JOSEPH (1859-1929) FRENCH
P/ 800
LAURENT, JEAN-ANTOINE (1763-1832) FRENCH
I/ 200
LAUSEN, UWE (B. 1941) ?
P/ 50-600
LAUTENSACK, HANS (1524-1560) GERMAN
I/ 145-23000
LAWRENCE, EDITH (1890-1973) BRITISH
R/ 450
LAWSON, ROBERT (1892-1957) AMERICAN
I/ 50-200
LAZZARI, PIETRO (B. 1898) AMERICAN
I/ 25-100
LAZZELL, BLANCHE (1878-1956) AMERICAN
P/ 990-3500   R/ 275-38500
LE BAS, JACQUES PHILIPPE (1707-1783) FRENCH
I/ 75-4600
LE FOLL, ALAIN (1935-1981) FRENCH
P/ 200
LE PAUTRE, JEAN (1618-1682) FRENCH
I/ 150-800
LEANDRE, CHARLES (1862-1930) FRENCH

P/ 125-600
LEBEGUE, LEON (19TH C) FRENCH
    P/ 350
LEBRUN, RICO (1900-1964) AMERICAN
    P/ 300
LECK, BART VAN DER (1876-1958) DUTCH
    P/ 700-2200
LEFEBRE, VALENTIN (1642-1680) FLEMISH
    I/ 75
LEFORT, HENRI (B. 1852) FRENCH
    I/ 60-175
LEFTROOK, TERRY (20TH C) AMERICAN
    I/ 80-150
LEGER, FERNAND (1881-1955) FRENCH
    I/ 200-11000   P/ 25-29000   R/ 1100
LEGRAND, LOUIS AUGUSTE MATHIEU (1863-1951) FRENCH
    I/ 25-2500
LEGROS, ALPHONSE (1837-1911) FRENCH
    I/ 15-400
LEHEUTRE, GUSTAVE (1861-1932) FRENCH
    I/ 50-835   P/ 330
LEHMANN-STEGLITZ (?) ?
    P/ 700
LEHMBRUCK, WILHELM (1881-1919) GERMAN
    I/ 150-13000   P/ 150-2300
LEHMDEN, ANTON (B. 1929) AUSTRIAN
    I/ 50-1800
LEIBIL, WILHELM (1844-1900) GERMAN
    I/ 100-2800
LEICH, CHESTER (B. 1889) AMERICAN
    I/ 25-100
LEIGH, HOWARD (B. 1896) AMERICAN
    P/ 50-100
LEIGHTON, CLARE (1899-1989) AMERICAN
    R/ 70-880
LEINBERGER, HANS (16TH C) GERMAN
    I/ 2800-3100
LEISTIKOW, WALTER (1865-1908) GERMAN
    I/ 100-1500   P/ 250-5800
LELONG, RENE (19TH/20TH C) FRENCH
    P/ 150-1000
LEMKE, HORST (?) ?
    I/ 800-1000   P/ 1000-1200
LEMMEL, CHARLES

P/ 125
LEMMEN, GEORGES (1865-1916) BELGIAN
   P/ 200-1500
LENEY, WILLIAM (1769-1831) BRITISH
   I/ 400
LENNON, JOHN (20TH C) BRITISH
   P/ 500
LENOIR, MARCEL (?) ?
   P/ 150-950
LEONART, JOHANN FRIEDRICH (1633-1680) GERMAN
   I/ 20-75
LEPARE, GEORGES (1887-1971) FRENCH
   P/ 200-8800
LEPERE, AUGUSTE (1849-1918) FRENCH
   I/ 50-2200   P/ 150-3100   R/ 100-2400
LEPICIE, NICOLAS BERNARD (1735-1784) FRENCH
   I/ 200-700
LEPRINCE, JEAN BAPTISTE (1734-1781) FRENCH
   I/ 50-600
LERICHIER, HENRI (20TH C) FRENCH
   I/ 30-75
LEROUX, GEORGES (B. 1877) FRENCH
   P/ 400-2400
LESSIEUX, LOUIS (?) ?
   P/ 1800
LEUPIN, HERBERT (?) ?
   P/ 60-800
LEUPPI, LEO PETER (1893-1972) DUTCH
   R/ 50-300
LEVER, HAYLEY (1876-1958) AMERICAN
   I/ 50-150
LEVINE, JACK (B. 1915) AMERICAN
   I/ 75-1800   P/ 50-1100
LEVINE, MARTIN (B. 1941) AMERICAN
   I/ 40-200
LEVY, ALPHONSE (1843-1918) FRENCH
   P/ 200-1650
LEVY, BEATRICE (1892-1974) AMERICAN
   I/ 200
LEWIS, ALLEN (1873-1957) AMERICAN
   R/ 30-175
LEWIS, MARTIN (1881-1962) AMERICAN
   I/ 200-19800   P/ 1100-8800
LEWITT, SOL (B. 1928) AMERICAN

- Prints at Auction -

I/ 25-1700   P/ 75-6000   R/ 2200
LEYDEN, LUCAS VAN (1494-1533) FLEMISH
   I/ 50-106000   R/ 180-96000
LEYMARIE, AUGUSTE (19TH/20TH C) FRENCH
   P/ 2000-3000
LHOTE, ANDRE (1885-1962) FRENCH
   I/ 300-550   P/ 150-1500   R/ 900
LICHTENSTEIN, ROY (B. 1923) AMERICAN
   I/ 1200-7700   P/ 200-82500   R/ 1400-44000
LIEBENWEIN, MAXIMILIEN (1869-1926) AUSTRIAN
   P/ 277-400
LIEBERMANN, MAX (1847-1935) GERMAN
   I/ 50-8900   P/ 50-6300   R/ 30-300
LIEVENS, JAN (1607-1674) DUTCH
   I/ 15-5700
LILLIE, ELLA FILLMORE (B. 1887) AMERICAN
   P/ 25-100
LIMBACH, RUSSELL (B. 1904) AMERICAN
   I/ 35-125   P/ 75-150
LINDENMUTH, TOD (1885-1976) AMERICAN
   R/ 300-2800
LINDNER, RICHARD (1901-1978) AMERICAN
   P/ 175-7200
LINDSAY, NORMAN ALFRED WILLIAMS (1879-1970) AUSTRALIAN
   I/ 500-1500
LINDSTROM, BENGT (B. 1925) SWEDISH
   I/ 100-350   P/ 250-400
LINGEE, CHARLES L. (1748-1819) FRENCH
   I/ 650
LIPCHITZ, JACQUES (1891-1973) FRENCH
   I/ 100-3900   P/ 210-1100
LIPINSKY, LINO S. (B. 1908) AMERICAN
   I/ 75-125
LIPS, JOHANN H. (1758-1817) SWISS
   I/ 100-250
LISSITZKY, EL (1890-1941) RUSSIAN
   P/ 100-62100
LITTLE, PHILIP (1857-1942) AMERICAN
   I/ 75-250
LIVEMONT, PRIVAT (1861-1936) BELGIAN
   P/ 300-7700
LOBEL-RICHE, ALMERY (B. 1880) FRENCH
   I/ 50-500
LOBISSER, SWITBERT (B. 1878) AUSTRIAN

R/ 100-500
LOCHOM, BARTOLOMEUS VAN (B. 1607) DUTCH
I/ 300
LOCKE, CHARLES WHEELER (1899-1983) AMERICAN
I/ 150   P/ 240-550
LOFFLER, BERTHOLD (1874-1960) AUSTRIAN
P/ 300-6300   R/ 1000
LOGAN, HERSCHEL C. (1901-1988) AMERICAN
R/ 100-250
LOHSE, RICHARD PAUL (B. 1902) SWISS
P/ 150-1000
LOLI, LORENZO (1612-1691) ITALIAN
I/ 40-1600
LONGO, ROBERT (B. 1953) AMERICAN
P/ 500-16000
LOO, ANDRE VAN (called CARLE VAN LOO) (1705-1765) FRENCH
I/ 150-600
LOPES-SILVA, LUCIEN (?) ?
P/ 1400
LORANT-HEILBRONN, V.
P/ 880-1000
LORCH, MELCHIOR (1527-1594) DANISH/GERMAN
I/ 400-32000
LORD, ELYSE ASHE (1900-1971) BRITISH
I/ 100-925
LORENZ, CARL (B. 1871) AUSTRIAN
R/ 25-225
LORENZI, GIOVANNI ANTONIO (1665-1740) ITALIAN
I/ 275-1100
LOSQUES, DANIEL DE (1880-1915) FRENCH
P/ 100-1400
LOUPOT, CHARLES (?) ?
P/ 650-18000
LOUTHERBOURG, JACQUES PHILIPP DE (1740-1812) FRENCH
I/ 350
LOUYS, PIERRE (?) ?
P/ 300-3500
LOZOWICK, LOUIS (1893-1973) AMERICAN
P/ 100-18700
LUBELL, WINIFRED M. (20TH C) AMERICAN
R/ 20-50
LUCAS, CHARLES E. (?) ?
P/ 300-2420
LUCE, MAXIMILIEN (1858-1941) FRENCH

I/ 200-800   P/ 75-5000
LUCIONI, LUIGI (B. 1900) AMERICAN
    I/ 50-525
LUGINBUHL, BERNHARD (B. 1929) SWISS
    I/ 200-3000   P/ 100-1300   R/ 125-3200
LUM, BERTHA BOYNTEN (1869-1954) AMERICAN
    R/ 240-1550
LUMSDEN, ERNEST STEPHEN (1883-1948) BRITISH
    I/ 50-500
LUNEL, FERDINAND (B. 1857) FRENCH
    P/ 275-4400
LUNOIS, ALEXANDRE (1863-1916) FRENCH
    I/ 95   P/ 25-950
LUPERTZ, MARKUS (B. 1941) GERMAN
    I/ 100-1300   P/ 60-1200   R/ 500-2900
LURCAT, JEAN (1892-1966) FRENCH
    I/ 50-600   P/ 100-500
LYDIS, MARIETTE RONSBERGER (1894-1970) AMERICAN
    I/ 50-125
LYON, ROLAND (1904-1966) AMERICAN
    R/ 25-100

M

MACARDELL, JAMES (1710-1765) BRITISH
    I/ 300-820
MACCOY, GUY (1904-1981) AMERICAN
    P/ 75-200
MACK, HEINZ (B. 1931) GERMAN
    I/ 300   P/ 100-2200
MACK, WARREN (B. 1896)
    I/ 25-100
MACKE, AUGUST (1887-1914) GERMAN
    R/ 800-4800   P/ 1765
MACKENSEN, FRITZ (B. 1866) GERMAN
    I/ 200-1500
MADRAZO, T.L.DE (?) ?
    P/ 250-2700
MAETZEL, EMIL (?) ?
    I/ 100-1000   P/ 90-1400   R/ 390-2400

Technique Key

Under each <u>printing technique</u> you may encounter the following types of prints (or combination of processes):

- **I** <u>Intaglio:</u>
  - etching
  - drypoint
  - steel engraving
  - stipple engraving
  - aquatint
  - mezzotint
  - soft-ground etching
  - crayon manner

- **P** <u>Planographic:</u>
  - lithograph
  - monotype
  - silk-screen
  - cliche verre
  - serigraph

- **R** <u>Relief:</u>
  - wood block
    - woodcut
      - chiaroscuro
    - wood engraving
  - linoleum cut (linocut)

MAETZEL-JOHANNSEN
    I/ 300-2500   R/ 200-900
MAGGIOTTO, FRANCESCO (1750-1805) ITALIAN
    I/ 250
MAGNELLI, ALBERTO (1888-1971) ITALIAN
    P/ 100-700   P/ 1450   R/ 200-900
MAGRITTE, RENE (1898-1967) BELGIAN
    I/ 200-10500   P/ 150-11000
MAHLER, HEINRICH (?) ?
    P/ 1000
MAIAKOVSKY, V. (?) ?
    P/ 225-1400
MAILLET, JACQUES L.(1823-1895) FRENCH
    I/ 100-300
MAILLOL, ARISTIDE (1861-1944) FRENCH
    I/ 100-1300   P/ 30-4000   R/ 25-12000
MAJOR, ISAAK (1576-1630) GERMAN
    I/ 900
MAKI, HAKU (20TH C) JAPANESE
    I/ 415   P/ 60-165   R/ 110
MAKS, CORNELIS JOHANNES (1876-1965) DUTCH
    P/ 400
MALETZKE, HELMUT (?) ?
    I/ 175   R/ 250
MALEVITCH, KASIMIR (1878-1935) RUSSIAN
    P/ 150-10520   R/ 350-2700
MALZAC, FRANC (?) ?
    P/ 750-900
MAN RAY, (1890-1976) AMERICAN
    I/ 50-2600   P/ 50-11000
MANASSER, TOBIAS (?) ?
    I/ 25-400
MANE-KATZ (1894-1962) FRENCH
    125-900
MANESSIER, ALFRED (B. 1911) FRENCH
    I/ 150-2800   P/ 50-2400
MANET, EDOUARD (1832-1883) FRENCH
    I/ 25-17000   P/ 600-187000
MANGOLD, BURKHARD (B. 1873) SWISS
    P/ 100-7300
MANGOLD, ROBERT (B. 1937) AMERICAN
    I/ 500-3300   P/ 100-1100   R/ 1100
MANGOLD, SILVIA P. (B. 1938) AMERICAN
    I/ 200-500

MANGUIN, HENRI CHARLES (1874-1943) FRENCH
I/ 200
MANTEGNA, ANDREA (1431-1506) ITALIAN
I/ 400-413000
MANZU, GIACOMO (B. 1908) ITALIAN
I/ 60-1300   P/ 400-1400
MARA, POL (B. 1920) BELGIAN
P/ 175-850
MARATTA, CARLO (1625-1713) ITALIAN
I/ 125-1700
MARC, FRANZ (1880-1916) GERMAN
P/ 2000-35000   R/ 100-42000
MARCA-RELLI, CONRAD (B. 1913) AMERICAN
P/ 100-600
MARCHAND, ANDRE (B. 1907) FRENCH
P/ 110-800
MARCHANT, LEONARD (20TH C) AMERICAN
I/ 50-150
MARCKS, GERHARD (B. 1889) GERMAN
I/ 125-475   P/ 100-6500   R/ 25-3200
MARCOUSSIS, LOUIS (1883-1941) FRENCH
I/ 50-73000   R/ 405
MARDEN, BRICE (B. 1938) AMERICAN
I/ 300-6600   P/ 275-6600
MARGOLIES, SAMUEL (1897-1974) AMERICAN
I/ 75-7700   P/ 50-550
MARGULIES, JOSEPH (1896-1984) AMERICAN
I/ 25-450
MARIANI, POMPEO (1857-1927) ITALIAN
P/ 300-11500 (monotypes only)
MARIESCHI, MICHELE (1710-1743) ITALIAN
I/ 150-6400
MARIN, JOHN (1872-1953) AMERICAN
I/ 200-57000
MARINI, MARINO (1901-1980) ITALIAN
I/ 60-7800   P/ 100-8800
MARISOL, ESCOBAR (B. 1930) AMERICAN
I/ 100-600   P/ 100-1350
MARKHAM, KYRA (1891-1967) AMERICAN
I/ 100-550   P/ 100-3025
MAROT, DANIEL (1663-1752) FRANCO/DUTCH
I/ 50-450
MARQUET, ALBERT (1875-1947) FRENCH
I/ 100-1900   P/ 25-3300   R/ 125-275

MARSH, REGINALD (1898-1954) AMERICAN
   I/ 200-22000   P/ 150-3500
MARTIN, CHARLES
   P/ 300-1100
MARTIN, HENRI (1860-1936) FRENCH
   P/ 250-2800
MARTIN, JOHN (1789-1854) BRITISH
   I/ 100-4000
MARTINET, FRANCOIS (18TH C) FRENCH
   I/ 300-1000
MARTINI, PIETRO A. (1739-1797) ITALIAN
   I/ 350-600
MARTSZ, de JONGE JAN (1609-after 1647) DUTCH
   I/ 100-600
MARTY, ANDRE E. (1882-1974) FRENCH
   P/ 750-1500
MARVAL, JACQUELINE (1866-1932) FRENCH
   P/ 200-350
MARYAN, MARYAN P/. B.(1927-1977) AMERICAN
   P/ 25-175
MASEREEL, FRANS (1889-1972) BELGIAN
   P/ 150-625   R/ 25-1900
MASIELLO, PASQUALE (B. 1912) AMERICAN
   I/ 25-100
MASOLLE, HELMER
   I/ 800-2000
MASON, RANDALL (?) ?
   I/ 300
MASSON, ANDRE (1896-1988) FRENCH
   I/ 60-15000   P/ 40-2000
MASTRO-VALERIO, ALESSANDRO (1887-1953) AMERICAN
   I/ 250-700
MATALONI, GIOVANNI
   P/ 1100-2000
MATANIA, FORTUNINO (B. 1881) ITALIAN
   P/ 1600-4200
MATARE, EWALD (1887-1965) GERMAN
   P/ 270   R/ 100-17050
MATHAM, ADRIAEN (1599-1660) DUTCH
   I/ 600
MATHAM, JACOB (1571-1631) DUTCH
   I/ 50-15700
MATHAM, THEODOR (1606-1676) DUTCH
   I/ 225-325

MATHIEU, GEORGES (B. 1921) FRENCH
    I/ 550   P/ 1060
MATISSE, HENRI (1869-1954) FRENCH
    I/ 100-137500   P/ 100-350000   R/ 175-46000
MATTA, ROBERTO ECHAUREN (B. 1912) CHILEAN
    I/ 50-1500   P/ 85-1000
MATTER, HERBERT
    P/ 650-11000
MATTHEUER, W.
    R/ 500-1200
MATULKA, JAN (1890-1972) CZECHOSLOVAKIAN/AMERICAN
    I/ 800-1500   P/ 990-25000
MAUFRA, MAXIME EMILE LOUIS (1861-1918) FRENCH
    I/ 220-3500   P/ 1000-4000
MAULBERTSCH, FRANZ ANTON (1742-1796) AUSTRIAN
    I/ 1000-2500
MAUPERCHE, HENRI (1602-1686) FRENCH
    I/ 400-450
MAURIN CHARLES (1856-1914) FRENCH
    I/ 50-3300   R/ 170
MAURONER, FABIO (B. 1884) ?
    I/ 50-100
MAUZAN, ACHILLE
    P/ 175-2700
MAUZEY, MERRITT (1898-1975) AMERICAN
    P/ 50-200
MAX, PETER (B. 1937) GERMAN/AMERICAN
    P/ 120-725
MAXIM, ORA INGE (1895-1982) AMERICAN
    R/ 3900
MAYER, MARTIN (1775-1821) FRENCH
    I/ 100-250   P/ 300
MAYHEW, NELL B. (20TH C) AMERICAN
    I/ 60-175
MAYO, EILEEN (?) ?
    R/ 350
MAZZOLA, FRANCESCO (called IL PARMIGIANIMO) (16TH C) ITALIAN
    I/ 2000-12000
MCALLISTER, ABEL F. (B. 1906) AMERICAN
    P/ 25-100   R/ 25-100
MCBEY, JAMES (1889-1959) BRITISH
    I/ 75-5300
MCCLOY, WILLIAM A. (B. 1913) AMERICAN
    I/ 25-100

MCCORMICK, HOWARD (1875-1943) AMERICAN
R/ 75-150
MCCORMICK, KATHERINE HOOD (1882-1960) AMERICAN
R/ 1200-2700
MCKINNIE, WENDALL (20TH C) AMERICAN
P/ 25-75
MCLEAN, BRUCE
P/ 300-2800
MCMILLEN, MILDRED (1884-1940) AMERICAN
R/ 350-800
MCNETT, WILLIAM B. (1896-1968) AMERICAN
P/ 25-100
MCNULTY, WILLIAM C. (1884-1963) AMERICAN
I/ 100-660
MCPHERSON, CRAIG (20TH C) AMERICAN
I/ 2000-5000
MECIKALSKI, EUGENE (B. 1927) AMERICAN
R/ 25-100
MECKENEM, ISRAEL VAN (D. 1503) GERMAN
I/ 500-71000
MECKSEPER, FRIEDRICH (B. 1936) GERMAN
I/ 60-3700   P/ 210   R/ 1900
MEER, JAN VAN DER (1656-1705) DUTCH
I/ 800
MEESER, LILLIAN BURK (1864-1942) AMERICAN
R/ 400
MEID, HANS (1883-1957) GERMAN
I/ 50-1100   P/ 15-500
MEIDNER, LUDWIG (1884-1966) GERMAN
I/ 55-2208   P/ 40-1700
MEIER, MELCHIOR (16TH/17TH C) SWISS
I/ 200-1700
MEISTERMANN, GEORG (B. 1911) GERMAN
I/ 500-1400   P/ 30-1220   R/ 500-1200
MELLAN, CLAUDE (1598-1688) FRENCH
I/ 150-6000
MELTZER, DORIS (B. 1908) AMERICAN
P/ 25-100
MELZER, MORITZ (B. 1877) GERMAN
I/ 800   P/ 690-3100   R/ 300-1650
MENPES, MORTIMER L. (1860-1938) BRITISH/AUSTRALIAN
I/ 50-1300
MENSE, CARL (1886-1965) GERMAN
I/ 200-650   P/ 100-500

MENZEL, ADOLF FRIEDRICH ERDMANN (1815-1905) GERMAN
I/ 50-650   P/ 25-3400   R/ 25-800
MERCATI, GIOVANNI-BATTISTA (B. 1600) ITALIAN
I/ 625
MERIAN, MATTHAUS (?) ?
I/ 25-3100
MERIDA, CARLOS (1891-1984) MEXICAN
P/ 25-900
MERRICK, RICHARD L. (B. 1903) AMERICAN
I/ 25-100
MERRILL, KATHARINE (B. 1896) AMERICAN
I/ 25-100
MERYON, CHARLES (1821-1868) FRENCH
I/ 100-52470
MESECK, FELIX (B. 1883) GERMAN
I/ 25-250
METIVET, LUCIEN (1863-1930) FRENCH
P/ 200-3600
METLICOVITZ, L.
P/ 150-11000
METZGER, CHARLES
P/ 750-1200
MEUNIER, GEORGES (B. 1869) FRENCH
P/ 100-1900
MEUNIER, HENRI (1873-1922) BELGIAN
I/ 300-350   P/ 450-3100
MEYER, FELIX (1653-1713) SWISS
I/ 250   P/ 300-600
MEYER-AMDEN, OTTO (B. 1885) SWISS
P/ 500-2000
MEYER-BASEL, CARL (1862-1932) SWISS
I/ 123-500   P/ 150
MICHAUX, HENRI (B. 1899) BELGIAN
I/ 650-1300   P/ 125-1400
MICHEL, ROBERT (B. 1897) GERMAN
I/ 800-1500   R/ 1500-3520
MIELE, JAN (1599-1663) FLEMISH
I/ 550-750
MIGNON, JEAN (16TH C) FRENCH
I/ 400-21000
MIKL, JOSEF (B. 1928) AUSTRIAN
P/ 350-450
MILAN, PIERRE (16TH C) FRENCH
I/ 700-7500

Technique Key

Under each <u>printing technique</u> you may encounter the following types of prints (or combination of processes):

- **I** <u>Intaglio:</u>
  - etching
  - drypoint
  - steel engraving
  - stipple engraving
  - aquatint
  - mezzotint
  - soft-ground etching
  - crayon manner

- **P** <u>Planographic:</u>
  - lithograph
  - monotype
  - silk-screen
  - cliche verre
  - serigraph

- **R** <u>Relief:</u>
  - wood block
    - woodcut
      - chiaroscuro
    - wood engraving
  - linoleum cut (linocut)

MILHOLLEN, HIRST D. (B. 1906) AMERICAN
I/ 25-100
MILLAIS, SIR JOHN EVERETT (1829-1896) BRITISH
I/ 100-990
MILLAR, FRED (?) ?
I/ 200
MILLER, HELEN P. (1888-1957) AMERICAN
I/ 25-100
MILLER, KENNETH HAYES (1876-1952) AMERICAN
I/ 125-600
MILLER, LEON GORDON (20TH C) AMERICAN
R/ 50-150
MILLER, RICHARD E. (B. 1875) AMERICAN
I/ 25-75
MILLET, JEAN FRANCOIS (1814-1875) FRENCH
I/ 200-26000   P/ 1100-19800
MILLIERE, MAURICE (B. 1871) FRENCH
I/ 175-12000   P/ 1600
MILSHTEIN, ZWI (B. 1934) ISRAELI
P/ 50-425
MILTON, PETER (B. 1930) AMERICAN
I/ 80-3900
MINAMI, KEIKO (B. 1911) JAPANESE
I/ 100-175
MINAUX, ANDRE (B. 1923) FRENCH
P/ 50-300
MINGUZZI, LUCIANO (B. 1911) ITALIAN
I/ 250-350
MINNE, GEORGE (1866-1941) BELGIAN
P/ 40-800
MINOR, ROBERT (1839-1904) AMERICAN
I/ 10-75
MIRER, RUDOLF
P/ 1700
MIRO, JOAN (1893-1983) SPANISH
I/ 100-165000   P/ 25-99000   R/ 100-27000
MISTI (19TH C) FRENCH
P/ 50-1200
MITELLI, GIUSEPPE 1634-1718) ITALIAN
I/ 325
MITCHELL, MARGUERITE (20TH C) AMERICAN
R/ 50-100
MITSCHKE-COLLANDE, CONSTANTIN VON (B. 1884) GERMAN
P/ 300

MOCK, GLADYS (B. 1892) AMERICAN
   I/ 25-100
MODENA, NICOLETTO DA (16TH C) ITALIAN
   I/ 500-16000
MODERSOHN-BECKER, PAULA (1876-1907) GERMAN
   I/ 1000-15000
MODIGLIANI, AMEDEO (1884-1920) ITALIAN
   I/ 300-900
MOFFETT, ROSS E. (B. 1888) AMERICAN
   P/ 75-250
MOHLITZ, PHILIPPE (B. 1941)
   I/ 125-825
MOHOLY-NAGY, LAZLO (1895-1946) HUNGARIAN/AMERICAN
   I/ 1500-3000   P/ 2000-37000   R/ 1000-15400
MOHRBUTTER, ALFRED (1867-1916) GERMAN
   P/ 150-800
MOLA, PIER FRANCESCO (1612-1666) ITALIAN
   I/ 650-700
MOLENAER, JAN M. (1610-1668) DUTCH
   I/ 1900
MOLIJN (MOLYN), PIETER (1595-1661) DUTCH
   I/ 100-1200
MOLKENBOER, T.H.A
   P/ 400-2400
MOLL, CARL (1861-1945) AUSTRIAN
   P/ 500-1100   R/ 50-1200
MOLOCH, B. (1849-1909) FRENCH
   P/ 175
MOLZAHN, JOHANNES (1892-1965) GERMAN
  p I/ 3476   P/ 2841   R/ 1600-3000
MONK, RICHARD BASIL
   R/ 200-400
MONNIER, HENRI DE (1805-1877) FRENCH
   P/ 60-2400
MONTAGNA, BENEDETTO (1481-1558) ITALIAN
   I/ 150-5400
MONVEL, BERNARD B.
   P/ 1100
MOORE, BENSON B. (B. 1882) AMERICAN
   I/ 25-100
MOORE, GEORGE BELTON (1805-1875) BRITISH
   P/ 250-400
MOORE, HENRY (1898-1986) BRITISH
   I/ 200-10000   P/ 30-22000   R/ 1500-15400

MOOS, MAX VON (B. 1903) ?
I/ 243   P/ 75-450   R/ 165
MORACH, OTTO (1887-1973) SWISS
P/ 1000-6100
MORAN, PETER (1841-1914) AMERICAN
I/ 75-300
MORAN, THOMAS (1837-1926) AMERICAN
I/ 100-3300   P/ 3300
MORANDI, GIORGIO (1890-1964) ITALIAN
I/ 1500-115500
MOREAU, JEAN M.(called MOREAU LE JEUNE) (1741-1814) FRENCH
I/ 200-1100
MOREAU, LUC-ALBERT (1882-1948) FRENCH
I/ 100   P/ 50-500
MOREAU, PIERRE LOUIS (B. 1876) FRENCH
I/ 50-300
MORELL, PIT (B. 1939) GERMAN
I/ 157-1500
MORETTI, LUCIEN PHILIPPE (20TH C) FRENCH
P/ 350-1500
MORGAN, FRANKLIN T. (B. 1883) AMERICAN
I/ 25-100
MORGAN, NORMA (B. 1928) AMERICAN
I/ 25-100
MORGNER, WILHELM (1891-1917) GERMAN
I/ 225-850   R/ 200-6000
MORIN, JEAN (1605-1650) FRENCH
I/ 125-2500
MORIN, LOUIS (B. 1855) FRENCH
P/ 400
MORISOT, BERTHE (1841-1895) FRENCH
I/ 90-1200
MORLAND, GEORGE (1763-1804) BRITISH
I/ 220-1600
MORLEY, EUGENE (1909-1953) AMERICAN
P/ 100-300
MORLEY, MALCOLM (B. 1931) BRITISH/AMERICAN
I/ 1000-2800   P/ 100-16500
MORO, BATTISTA ANGOLO DEL (1514-1573) ITALIAN
I/ 725
MORRIS, ROBERT (B. 1931) AMERICAN
P/ 50-550
MORPER, DANIEL (B. 1937) AMERICAN
P/ 150-425

MORTENSEN, RICHARD (B. 1910) DANISH
P/ 80-600
MOSER, KOLOMON (1868-1918) AUSTRIAN
P/ 390-22000
MOSES, ED (B. 1926) AMERICAN
P/ 300-1320
MOSKOWITZ, ROBERT (B. 1935) AMERICAN
P/ 1000-2500   R/ 1650
MOTHERWELL, ROBERT (B. 1915) AMERICAN
I/ 175-26000   P/ 175-63400
MOUEL, EUGENE LE
P/ 200-1200
MOYREAU, JEAN (1690-1762) FRENCH
I/ 200-500
MUCHA, ALPHONSE MARIA (1860-1939) CZECHOSLOVAKIAN
P/ 25-52800
MUCHE, GEORG (B. 1895) GERMAN
I/ 350-2300   R/ 3650
MUCK, FRIEDRICH O. (19TH/20TH C) GERMAN
P/ 50-100
MUELLER, HANS A. (1888-1962) AMERICAN
R/ 40-75
MUGGIANI, GIORGIO
P/ 900-2400
MUHLENHAUPT, CURT
I/ 150-275   P/ 100-200   R/ 75-275
MULLER, ALBERT (B. 1884) GERMAN
I/ 300-1900   R/ 600-2000
MULLER, ALFREDO (B. 1869) ITALIAN
I/ 300-1300   P/ 200-1000
MULLER, C.O.
P/ 125-200   R/ 1800-3000
MULLER, FRIEDRICH (1782-1816)
I/ 200-1200
MULLER, JAN HARMENSZ (1571-1628) DUTCH
I/ 50-9400   P/ 500
MUELLER, OTTO (1874-1930) GERMAN
P/ 60-95500   R/ 600-9500
MULLER, RICHARD (1874-1930) AUSTRIAN
I/ 25-1000   P/ 300
MULLER-LINOW, BRUNO (B. 1925) SWISS
I/ 200-275   P/ 360
MUNAKATA, SHIKO (1903-1975) JAPANESE
R/ 130-132000

MUNCH, EDVARD (1863-1944) NORWEGIAN
 I/ 75-56300   P/ 145-616000   R/ 3600-187000
MUNCH-KHE, WILLI (B. 1885) GERMAN
 I/ 50-250
MUNTER, GABRIELE (1877-1962) GERMAN
 I/ 2500   P/ 380-1200   R/ 3900
MURPHY, ALICE HAROLD (1896-1966) AMERICAN
 P/ 30-150
MURPHY, CATHERINE (B. 1946) AMERICAN
 P/ 100-500
MURRAY, ELIZABETH (B. 1940) AMERICAN
 P/ 380-9900
MUSI, AGOSTINO DEI (1490-1540) ITALIAN
 I/ 250-5600
MUSIC, ZORAN ANTONIO (1909-1952) ITALIAN
 I/ 30-1700   P/ 50-3700

N

NAGEL, PIETER (B. 1941) DUTCH
 I/ 70-525   P/ 200-880
NAGELE, REINHOLD (20TH C) ?
 I/ 100-600
NALBANDIAN, KARNIG (B. 1916) AMERICAN
 I/ 25-100
NAMIKI, HAJIME
 R/ 600
NARDOIS, JEAN G.
 I/ 800-1400
NASH, PAUL (1889-1946) BRITISH
 I/ 5200   P/ 550-5300   R/ 100-1100
NASH, WILLARD AYER (1898-1943) AMERICAN
 P/ 175-550
NASON, GERTRUDE (1890-1969) AMERICAN
 R/ 100-250
NASON, THOMAS (1889-1971) AMERICAN
 I/ 75-280   R/ 200-300
NATKIN, ROBERT (B. 1930) AMERICAN
 P/ 100-1200   I/ 1700-1800
NAUEN, HEINRICH (1880-1940) GERMAN

I/ 375-3100
NAUMAN, BRUCE (B. 1941) AMERICAN
I/ 400-5000   P/ 250-16500
NAUMANN, HERMANN
I/ 35   P/ 75-9100
NAVARRO, F.DE
P/ 1300
NAY, ERNST WILHELM (1902-1968) GERMAN
I/ 30-15600   P/ 175-14000   R/ 200-1500
NEAL, REGINALD (B. 1909) AMERICAN
P/ 75-650
NEBEL, OTTO (B. 1892) SWISS
P/ 225   R/ 50-700
NEEFFS, JACOBUS (1610-1660) DUTCH
I/ 125-400
NEEL, ALICE (1901-1984) AMERICAN
P/ 300-1800
NERI, MANUEL (B. 1930) AMERICAN
P/ 800
NESBITT, JACKSON LEE (B. 1913) AMERICAN
I/ 75-495
NESBITT, LOWELL (B. 1933) AMERICAN
P/ 50-550
NESCH, ROLF (B. 1893) GERMAN
I/ 175-33000   P/ 200-9900   R/ 1000-1700
NEUKOMM, FRED
P/ 800
NEUMANN, HANS (B. 1873) GERMAN
P/ 770   R/ 200-700
NEVE, FRANS DE (1606-1681) FLEMISH
I/ 150-200
NEVELSON, LOUISE (1900-1988) AMERICAN
I/ 500-8250   P/ 50-2000
NEVINSON, CHRISTOPHER RICHARD WYNNE (1889-1946) BRITISH
I/ 150-10800   P/ 250-9200
NEWMAN, BARNETT (1905-1970) AMERICAN
I/ 1400-20000   P/ 1500-66000
NEWMAN, JOHN
I/ 1320   P/ 1000-1870
NEWTON, EDITH W. (B. 1878) AMERICAN
P/ 25-100
NEZIERE, J.DE LA (?) ?
P/ 325-500
NICHOLS, DALE WILLIAM (B. 1904) AMERICAN

Technique Key

Under each <u>printing technique</u> you may encounter the following types of prints (or combination of processes):

- **I** <u>Intaglio:</u>
  - etching
  - drypoint
  - steel engraving
  - stipple engraving
  - aquatint
  - mezzotint
  - soft-ground etching
  - crayon manner

- **P** <u>Planographic:</u>
  - lithograph
  - monotype
  - silk-screen
  - cliche verre
  - serigraph

- **R** <u>Relief:</u>
  - wood block
    - woodcut
      - chiaroscuro
    - wood engraving
  - linoleum cut (linocut)

P/ 75-660
NICHOLSON, BEN (1894-1982) BRITISH
    I/ 75-8300   P/ 955   R/ 300-9000
NICHOLSON, SIR WILLIAM (1872-1949) BRITISH
    I/ 300   P/ 50-7700   R/ 25-5000
NILSON, JOHANN E. (1799-1867) GERMAN
    I/ 200-250
NISBET, ROBERT HOGG (1879-1961) AMERICAN
    I/ 20-125
NITTIS, GIUSEPPE DE (1846-1884) ITALIAN
    I/ 250
NIZZOLI, MARCELLO
    P/ 250-6600
NODA, TETSUYA (B. 1940) JAPANESE
    R/ 600-700
NOEL, GUY-GERARD
    P/ 900-1800
NOLAND, KENNETH (B. 1924) AMERICAN
    I/ 1600-11000   P/ 400-31000
NOLDE, EMIL (1867-1956) GERMAN
    I/ 300-48000   P/ 175-258000   R/ 100-62700
NOLKEN, FRANZ (B. 1884) GERMAN
    I/ 100-1100
NOLPE, PIETER (1613-1652) DUTCH
    I/ 200
NOMELLINI, PLINIO (1866-1943) ITALIAN
    P/ 1200
NORBLIN, STEFAN (B. 1892)
    P/ 600
NORDFELDT, BROR JULIUS O. (1878-1955) AMERICAN
    I/ 150-330   R/ 1100-15400
NOTHNAGEL, JOHANNES ANDREAS BENJAMIN (1729-1804) GERMAN
    I/ 75-200
NOURY, GASTON (B. 1866) FRENCH
    P/ 200
NOVAK, LOUIS (B. 1903) AMERICAN
    R/ 75-300
NOVELLANUS, A. (17TH C) GERMAN
    I/ 500
NUANCE, WALTER (20TH C) AMERICAN
    P/ 50-100
NUTTING, MYRON C. (B. 1890) AMERICAN
    P/ 25-100

O

O'CONNOR, RODERICK (1860-1940) IRISH
I/ 100-3500
O'GALOP (19TH C) FRENCH
P/ 225-1500
O'HIGGINS, PABLO (B. 1904) AMERICAN
P/ 75-175   R/ 880
O'KEEFE, IDA T.E. (B. 1899) AMERICAN
I/ 100-200
OAKFORD, ELLEN (19TH C) AMERICAN
I/ 50-150
OBERMEIER, OTTO (B. 1883) GERMAN
P/ 350-1900
OCHOA, R. DE (?) ?
P/ 250-300
OFFIN, CHARLES Z. (B. 1899) AMERICAN
I/ 40-100
OGE, E. (19TH C) FRENCH
P/ 200-1800
OGUISS, TAKANARI (B. 1900) JAPANESE
P/ 500-2800
OHCHI, HIROSHI
P/ 700
OLBRICH, JOSEPH M. (1867-1908) AUSTRIAN
P/ 2100-10000
OLDE, HANS (1855-1917) GERMAN
I/ 250
OLDENBURG, CLAES THURE (B. 1929) AMERICAN
I/ 275-71500   P/ 50-23000
OLITSKI, JULES (1922-1964) AMERICAN
P/ 175-2000
OLIVEIRA, NATHAN (B. 1928) AMERICAN
I/ 200-1200   P/ 200-4000
OLIVER, PETER (1594-1647) BRITISH
I/ 3300-13000
OLIVIER, FERDINAND J. H. VON (1785-1841) GERMAN
P/ 600-18000
OLMUTZ, WENZEL VON OLSKY
I/ 100-2300
ONOFRI, CESARE (1632-1712) ITALIAN
I/ 600-1200
OPITZ, FRANZ KARL

I/ 250
OPPENHEIM, DENNIS A. (B. 1938) AMERICAN
P/ 50-500
OPPENHEIM, LOUIS (19TH C) GERMAN
P/ 250-4000
OPPENHEIM, MERET (B. 1913) SWISS
P/ 100-4000   R/ 465
OPPENHEIMER, MAX (called MOPP) (1885-1954) GERMAN
I/ 25-850   P/ 150-2200   R/ 475
OPPLER, ERNST (B. 1869) GERMAN
I/ 25-650   P/ 200-300
ORAZI, MANUEL (19TH/20TH C) FRENCH
P/ 50-28000
ORGAN, BRYAN (B. 1935) BRITISH
P/ 100-500
ORLEY, RICHARD VAN (?) ?
I/ 88-700
ORLIK, EMIL (1879-1932) CZECHOSLOVAKIAN
I/ 90-1700   P/ 25-1200   R/ 100-5000
OROZCO, JOSE CLEMENTE (1883-1949) MEXICAN
I/ 30-1100   P/ 40-7500
ORSI, (?) ?
P/ 500-13000
ORTEGA, JOSE (B. 1940) SPANISH
I/ 75-650
OSIECKI, STEFAN
P/ 450
OSSENBEECK, JAN VAN (1624-1674) DUTCH
I/ 250-1400
OSTADE, ADRIAEN VAN (1610-1679) DUTCH
I/ 25-47000   R/ 40
OSTADE, ISAAC VAN (1621-1649) DUTCH
I/ 725
OSTENDORFER, MARTIN (16TH C) GERMAN
R/ 100-5400
OSTERLIND, ANDERS (1887-1960) FRENCH
I/ 175-400
OSTROWSKY, ABBO (B. 1889) AMERICAN
I/ 70-100
OTTO, HEINRICH
I/ 100-475
OUDRY, JEAN BAPTISTE (1686-1755) FRENCH
I/ 300-1900
OURY, LEON LOUIS (B. 1846) FRENCH

P/ 230-1000
OUTGERSZ, WILLEM
    I/ 425-1200
OVERBECK, FRITZ (1869-1909) GERMAN
    I/ 200-800
OWEN, FREDERICK L. (1869-1959) CANADIAN
    I/ 15-60

P

PAESCHKE, PAUL (B. 1875) GERMAN
    I/ 75-800   P/ 400-1700
PAL (20TH C)
    P/ 75-2700
PALADINO, MIMMO (B. 1948) ITALIAN
    I/ 30-12100   P/ 300-4800   R/ 550-3700
PALAZUELO, PABLO (B. 1916) SPANISH
    I/ 200-500
PALERMO, BLINKY (?) ?
    P/ 350-5300
PALING, RICHARD (B. 1901) GERMAN
    I/ 350
PALM, JOACHIM (?) ?
    I/ 50-125
PALMA, JACOPO (called IL GIOVANE) (1544-1628) ITALIAN
    I/ 50-1800
PALMER, SAMUEL (1805-1881) BRITISH
    I/ 100-11900   R/ 4530
PANAMARENKO (B. 1940) BELGIAN
    P/ 275-2000
PANDEREN, EGBERT (1581-1637) DUTCH
    I/ 300
PANKOK, BERNHARD (B. 1872) GERMAN
    I/ 341   P/ 150-425
PANKOK, OTTO (20TH C) ?
    I/ 200-2900   P/ 100-2200   R/ 250-3000
PAOLOZZI, EDUARDO (B. 1924) BRITISH
    I/ 200-350   P/ 25-600
PAPART, MAX (B. 1911) FRENCH
    I/ 400-800   P/ 100-600

PAPPRILL, HENRY (19TH C) AMERICAN
I/ 3300-9900
PARMIGIANINO, FRANCESCO MAZZOLA (1503-1540) ITALIAN
I/ 200-12000   R/ 6000-11000
PARRISH, CLARA WAEVER (D. 1925) AMERICAN
I/ 40-75
PARRISH, STEPHEN WINDSOR (1846-1938) AMERICAN
I/ 75-500
PARROCEL, CHARLES (1688-1752) FRENCH
I/ 30-1500
PARTRIDGE, ROY (1888-1984) AMERICAN
I/ 100-1600
PARZINGER, HANS
P/ 2400
PASCHKE, ED (B. 1938) AMERICAN
P/ 100-1760
PASCIN, JULES (1885-1930) AMERICAN
I/ 130-2300   P/ 25-1000
PASMORE, VICTOR (B. 1908) BRITISH
I/ 175-3300   P/ 100-1000
PASSAROTTI, BARTOLOMEO (1529-1592) ITALIAN
I/ 250-5000
PASSE, CRISPIJN VAN DE II (c. 1590-1670) DUTCH
I/ 50-1200
PASSE, MAGDALENA DE (1600-1638) DUTCH
I/ 440-850
PASSERI, BERNARDINO (16TH C) ?
I/ 3000
PATEK, AUGUST
P/ 1600
PATER, JEAN BAPTISTE (1695-1736) FRENCH
I/ 275
PATTERSON, MARGARET JORDAN (1867-1950) AMERICAN
I/ 165   P/ 220   R/ 100-4000
PAUL, HERMANN RENE GEORGE (1864-1940) FRENCH
P/ 700-4400
PAUL, PETER (1865-1937) BRITISH
P/ 50-300
PAULI, FRITZ EDUARD (1891-1968) SWISS
I/ 100-900   P/ 319
PAULL, GRACE A. (B. 1898) AMERICAN
P/ 25-100
PAULOZZI, EDUARDO (20TH C) AMERICAN
P/ 80-175

PAULSEN, INGWER (B. 1883) GERMAN
    I/ 100-400
PAUNZEN, ARTHUR (B. 1890) AUSTRIAN
    I/ 20-80
PAVIL, ELIE ANATOLE (1873-1948) FRENCH
    P/ 200-1200
PEALE, CHARLES WILSON (1741-1827) AMERICAN
    I/ 8800
PEAN, RENE (20TH C) FRENCH
    P/ 200-1600
PEARLSTEIN, PHILIP (B. 1924) AMERICAN
    I/ 150-9900   P/ 150-5300
PEARS, CHARLES (1873-1958) BRITISH
    P/ 500-1900
PEARSON, JOHN (20TH C) AMERICAN
    P/ 25-75
PEARSON, RALPH M. (1883-1958) AMERICAN
    I/ 25-100
PECHE, DAGOBERT (1887-1923) AUSTRIAN
    P/ 200-6200
PECHSTEIN, MAX HERMANN M. (1881-1955) GERMAN
    I/ 250-14300   P/ 100-28000   R/ 160-83000
PECK, HENRY J. (1880-1964) AMERICAN
    I/ 40-125
PEET, ORVILLE HOUGHTEEN (1884-1968) AMERICAN
    I/ 40-100
PEETS, ORVILLE H. (B. 1884-1968) AMERICAN
    I/ 25-100
PEIFFER-WATENPHUL, MAX (B. 1896) GERMAN
    I/ 30-400   P/ 100-1800
PENCK, A. R. (B. 1939) GERMAN
    I/ 25-4600   P/ 60-6200   R/ 800-2000
PENCZ, GEORG (1500-1550) GERMAN
    I/ 75-6000
PENFIELD, EDWARD (1866-1925) AMERICAN
    P/ 100-7700
PENNELL, JOSEPH (1857-1926) AMERICAN
    I/ 25-4600   P/ 50-700
PEPPER, BEVERLY (B. 1924) AMERICAN
    P/ 3500
PEPPER, CHARLES HOVEY (1864-1950) AMERICAN
    R/ 175-250
PERISSIM, J.J. (?) ?
    I/ 950

Technique Key

Under each <u>printing technique</u> you may encounter the following types of prints (or combination of processes):

- **I** <u>Intaglio:</u>
  - etching
  - drypoint
  - steel engraving
  - stipple engraving
  - aquatint
  - mezzotint
  - soft-ground etching
  - crayon manner

- **P** <u>Planographic:</u>
  - lithograph
  - monotype
  - silk-screen
  - cliche verre
  - serigraph

- **R** <u>Relief:</u>
  - wood block
    - woodcut
      - chiaroscuro
    - wood engraving
  - linoleum cut (linocut)

PESCHERET, LEON R. (1892-1961) AMERICAN
I/ 40-75
PESKE, JEAN (1880-1949) FRENCH
P/ 5000-7700
PETERDI, GABOR (B. 1915) HUNGARIAN
I/ 50-400
PETTIJEAN, EDMOND MARIE (1844-1925) FRENCH
P/ 150-900
PFAFF, HANS (B. 1875) GERMAN
P/ 800-1900
PHILBRICK, MARGARET E. (B. 1914) AMERICAN
I/ 25-100
PHILBRICK, OTIS (1888-1973) AMERICAN
P/ 25-100
PHILIPPI, ROBERT (?) ?
R/ 25-400
PHILLIPS, MATT (B. 1927) AMERICAN
I/ 315   P/ 150-700
PHILLIPS, PETER (B. 1939) BRITISH
P/ 60-500
PHILLIPS, WALTER JOSEPH (1884-1963) CANADIAN
R/ 300-5600
PIAUBERT, JEAN (B. 1900) FRENCH
P/ 220-550
PIAZZETTA, GIAMBATTISTA (1682-1754) ITALIAN
I/ 200-2200
PICASSO, PABLO (1881-1973) SPANISH
I/ 190-1750100   P/ 25-248000   R/ 35-457600
PICCIONI, MATTEO (1615-1671) ITALIAN
I/ 450
PICKING, H.
P/ 1700
PIEKERT, MARTIN
P/ 700
PIENE, OTTO (B. 1928) GERMAN
P/ 100-600   R/ 500
PIERCE, LEONA (B. 1922) AMERICAN
R/ 25-100
PIGNON, EDOUARD (B. 1905) FRENCH
I/ 250-300   P/ 150-400
PIPER, JOHN (1903-1992) BRITISH
I/ 50-1700   P/ 40-1700
PIRANESI, FRANCESCO (1758-1810) ITALIAN
I/ 90-6500

PIRANESI, GIOVANNI-BATTISTA (1720-1778) ITALIAN
I/ 200-56300
PIRSON, ELMER W. (B. 1888) AMERICAN
P/ 1200
PISSARRO, CAMILLE (1830-1903) FRENCH
I/ 40-107000   P/ 500-89500
PISSARRO, GEORGE HENRI (1871-1961) FRENCH
I/ 400   P/ 300-600
PISSARRO, LUCIEN (1863-1944) FRENCH
P/ 300-1000   R/ 100-1200
PISSARRO, OROVIDA (B. 1893) FRENCH
I/ 100-400   R/ 531
PISTOLETTO, MICHELANGELO (B. 1933) ITALIAN
P/ 475-8000
PITZ, HENRY C. (1895-1976) AMERICAN
P/ 25-100
PIZ, GEORG EMANUEL (?) ?
I/ 1000
PIZA, ARTHUR LUIZ (B. 1928) BRAZILIAN
I/ 100-800
PLANSON, ANDRE (1898-1981) FRENCH
P/ 25-350
PLASSARD, VINCENT (17TH C) FRENCH
I/ 300
PLATSCHEK, HANS (B. 1923) GERMAN
P/ 50-400
PLATTENBERG, MATHIAS VAN (1608-1660) ?
I/ 300-900
PLOOS VAN AMSTEL, C. (1726-1798) DUTCH
I/ 200-2600
PLOWMAN, GEORGE TAYLOR (1869-1932) AMERICAN
I/ 30-150
PLUNNECKE, WILHELM (B. 1894) GERMAN
P/ 25-150
PODESTA, GIOVANNI (1620-1674) ITALIAN
I/ 375-3100
POLANZINI, R. (?) ?
I/ 500
POLIAKOFF, SERGE (1906-1969) FRENCH
I/ 200-11000   P/ 100-14300
POLKE, SIGMAR (B. 1941) GERMAN
P/ 250-40000
POLLAK, MAX (1886-1970) AUSTRIAN
I/ 100-1200

POLLARD, JAMES (1797-1859) BRITISH
I/ 125-2000
POLLARD, ROBERT (1755-1838) BRITISH
I/ 500
POLLEY, FREDERICK (1875-1958) AMERICAN
I/ 30-90
POLLOCK, JACKSON (1912-1956) AMERICAN
I/ 7700-8800   P/ 800-23100
POLO, LUISA (?) ?
P/ 550
POLSTER, DORA (B. 1884) GERMAN
P/ 700
POMODORO, ARNOLDO (B. 1926) ITALIAN
P/ 125-1800
PONT, CHARLES E. (B. 1898) AMERICAN
R/ 25-100
PONTIUS, PAULUS (1603-1658) FLEMISH
I/ 200-950
PONTY, MAX (?) ?
P/ 200-14000
POONS, LARRY (B. 1937) AMERICAN
P/ 220-400
PORTER, FAIRFIELD (1907-1975) AMERICAN
P/ 55-1400
POTTHOF, HANS (?) ?
P/ 150-850
POUGNY, JEAN (1894-1956) FRENCH
P/ 60-3600
POUSSIN, ETIENNE DE (?) ?
I/ 50
POWER, CYRIL (1875-1951) BRITISH
I/ 335   P/ 430-2100   R/ 100-12600
POZZATTI, RUDY (B. 1925) AMERICAN
I/ 75-200
PRAMPOLINI, ENRICO (1894-1956) ITALIAN
P/ 550-1600
PREETORIUS, EMIL (B. 1883) GERMAN
P/ 400-2600
PREISS, FRITZ (B. 1883) GERMAN
P/ 300-350
PREM, HEIMRAD (B. 1934) GERMAN
P/ 200-800   R/ 220
PRENDERGAST, MAURICE BRAZIL (1859-1924) AMERICAN
P/ 55000-182000 (monotypes only)

PRICE, KEN (B. 1935) AMERICAN
  P/ 150-1500
PRICE, NICK (?) ?
  P/ 850-5900
PRIEST, HARTWELL W. (B. 1901) AMERICAN
  I/ 25-100
PRIOR, CHARLES M. (B. 1865) AMERICAN
  I/ 25-100
PRIOR, MARNA A. (20TH C) AMERICAN
  P/ 10-50
PROCACCINI, CAMILLO (1550-1629) ITALIAN
  I/ 200-23000
PROCKTOR, PATRICK (20TH C) BRITISH
  I/ 50-550   P/ 70-775
PRUD'HON, PIERRE PAUL (1758-1823) FRENCH
  P/ 400-2400
PRUNIERE, J. (1901-1944) FRENCH
  P/ 100-300
PUCHINGER, ERWIN (B. 1876) AUSTRIAN
  P/ 3000
PUGH, SARAH M. (B. 1891) AMERICAN
  P/ 25-100   R/ 25-100
PULLINGER, HERBERT (B. 1878) AMERICAN
  I/ 50-125
PURRMANN, HANS (1880-1966) GERMAN
  I/ 100-1900   P/ 80-1000   R/ 517
PURVIS, TOM
  P/ 800-6000
PYROTH, CHRISTA
  I/ 100-600   P/ 175

Q

QUAGLIO, DOMENICO (1786-1837) GERMAN
  I/ 1025   P/ 90-350
QUAST, PIETER JANSZ (1605-1647) DUTCH
  I/ 140-600
QUINTE, LOTHAR (B. 1923) GERMAN
  P/ 100-950

R

RABINOVICH, GREGOR (B. 1884) RUSSIAN
    I/ 30-300   P/ 25
RABOY, MAC (B. 1914) AMERICAN
    R/ 25-100
RAEMAEKERS, LOUIS (1869-1956) DUTCH
    P/ 1000-2400
RAETZ, MARKUS (B. 1941) SWISS
    I/ 300-650   P/ 485
RAFFAEL, JOSEPH (B. 1933) AMERICAN
    P/ 300-3850   R/ 550
RAFFAELLI, JEAN FRANCOIS (1850-1924) FRENCH
    I/ 100-5000   P/ 175-300
RAIMONDI, MARCANTONIO (1480-1534) ITALIAN
    I/ 50-33000
RAINER, ARNULF (B. 1929) AUSTRIAN
    I/ 100-4200   P/ 50-6000
RAMOS, MEL (B. 1935) AMERICAN
    P/ 75-2670
RAMSDELL, FRED WINTHROP (1865-1915) AMERICAN
    P/ 700-2300
RAMUS, CHARLES F. (B. 1902) AMERICAN
    P/ 40-90
RANFT, RICHARD (1862-1931) SWISS
    I/ 300-1100
RANSON, PAUL (1864-1909) FRENCH
    P/ 275-11000
RASMUSSEN, AAGE
    P/ 880-1200
RASSENFOSSE, ARMAND (1862-1934) BELGIAN
    P/ 50-5300
RATTNER, ABRAHAM (1895-1978) AMERICAN
    P/ 60-200
RAUSCHENBERG, ROBERT (B. 1925) AMERICAN
    I/ 500-7700   P/ 100-176000
RAVENNA, MARCO DA (DENTE) (D. 1527) ITALIAN
    I/ 1000-5200
RAVENSCROFT, ELLEN (1876-1949) AMERICAN
    R/ 1300-1900
RAY, MAN (see MAN RAY) AMERICAN
READ, DAVID CHARLES (1790-1851) BRITISH
    I/ 15-100

REBEYROLLE, PAUL (B. 1926) FRENCH
P/ 180-500
RECKZIEGEL, ANTON (B. 1865) AUSTRIAN
P/ 275
REDDY, KRISHNA (B. 1925) AMERICAN
I/ 200
REDON, GEORGES (1869-1943) FRENCH
I/ 200   P/ 400-2000
REDON, ODILON (1840-1916) FRENCH
I/ 260-13200   P/ 40-80000
REED, EARL H. (1863-1931) AMERICAN
I/ 25-100
REED, ETHEL (B. 1876) AMERICAN
P/ 300-1700
REEVES, RUTH (B. 1892) AMERICAN
I/ 25
REIBER, RICHARD H. (B. 1912) AMERICAN
I/ 50-125
REICHERT, JOSUA
R/ 225-275
REID, JAMES (B. 1907) AMERICAN
P/ 25-100
REIMER, LUDWIG C.
I/ 600
REINBOLD, ANTON (B. 1881) GERMAN
P/ 1200
REINDEL, WILLIAM G. (1871-1948) AMERICAN
I/ 40-75
REINHARDT, AD (1913-1967) AMERICAN
P/ 100-935
REINHART, JOHANN CHRISTIAN (1761-1847) GERMAN
I/ 100-2900
REMBRANDT, (REMBRANDT HARMENSZ VAN RIJN) (1606-1669) DUTCH
I/ 50-999000
RENAULT, ABEL PIERRE (B. 1903) FRENCH
P/ 225
RENESSE, CONSTANTIJN DANIEL VON (1626-1680) DUTCII
I/ 250-6500
RENI, GUIDO (1575-1642) ITALIAN
I/ 150-3500
RENOIR, PIERRE AUGUSTE (1841-1919) FRENCH
I/ 35-19500   P/ 30-193600
RENOUF, EDDA (B. 1943) MEXICAN/AMERICAN
I/ 100-150

Technique Key

Under each <u>printing technique</u> you may encounter the following types of prints (or combination of processes):

- **I** <u>Intaglio:</u>
  - etching
  - drypoint
  - steel engraving
  - stipple engraving
  - aquatint
  - mezzotint
  - soft-ground etching
  - crayon manner

- **P** <u>Planographic:</u>
  - lithograph
  - monotype
  - silk-screen
  - cliche verre
  - serigraph

- **R** <u>Relief:</u>
  - wood block
    - woodcut
      - chiaroscuro
    - wood engraving
  - linoleum cut (linocut)

I/ 25-80
WILSON, EDWARD A. (1886-1970) AMERICAN
P/ 50-300
WILSON, JOHN (B. 1922) AMERICAN
P/ 100-550
WILSON, ROBERT BURNS (1851-1916) AMERICAN
I/ 970   P/ 200-690
WILTZ, ARNOLD (1889-1937) AMERICAN
I/ 75-150   P/ 30-75
WIMMER, PAULA
R/ 25-600
WINCKLE, F. (B. 1766) AUSTRIAN
P/ 600
WINKLER, JOHN W. (1890-1979) AMERICAN
I/ 75-500
WINNER, GERD (B. 1936) GERMAN
P/ 150-2000
WINNEWISSER, ROLF (B. 1949) SWISS
R/ 100
WINSLOW, HENRY (1874-1955) AMERICAN
I/ 25-100
WINTER, FRITZ (1905-1978) GERMAN
I/ 100-3300   P/ 100-2050
WINTERS, TERRY (B. 1939) AMERICAN
I/ 3850   P/ 385-25300
WIRSCHING, OTTO (1889-1919) GERMAN
R/ 25
WITHERSTINE, DONALD (1896-1961) AMERICAN
R/ 20-75
WOEHRMAN, RALPH
I/ 50-275
WOELFFNER, EMERSON (B. 1914) AMERICAN
P/ 350
WOLF, HENRY (1852-1916) AMERICAN
I/ 30-75
WOLFGANG, GUSTAV A. (1692-1775) GERMAN
I/ 400
WOLFGANG, JOHANN G. (1662-1744) GERMAN
I/ 275
WOLFSFELD, ERICH (B. 1884)
I/ 300
WOLFSON, WILLIAM (B. 1894) AMERICAN
I/ 275   P/ 1000-2000
WOLGEMUT, MICHAEL (1434-1519) GERMAN

R/ 250-800
WOLLHEIM, GERT H. (?) ?
    I/ 950   R/ 200-5800
WOLS, (ALFRED O. W. S.) (1913-1951) GERMAN
    I/ 150-600
WOMRATH, ANDREW (B. 1869) AMERICAN
    I/ 500   P/ 200-1300
WOOD, GRANT (1891-1942) AMERICAN
    P/ 400-6600
WOODBURY, CHARLES HERBERT (1864-1940) AMERICAN
    I/ 80-450
WOODWARD, ELLSWORTH (1861-1939) AMERICAN
    I/ 25-100
WOODWARD, STANLEY (B. 1894) AMERICAN
    I/ 25-100
WOOLF, SAMUEL J. (1880-1948) AMERICAN
    P/ 80-175
WORN, WALTER (?) ?
    P/ 100-650   R/ 50-1200
WOTRUBA, FRITZ (1907-1975) GERMAN
    I/ 75-700   P/ 50-1800
WRIGHT, REDMOND S. (B. 1903) AMERICAN
    I/ 25-100
WRIGHT, STANTON M. (20TH C) AMERICAN
    R/ 100-500
WUCHERER, FRITZ (B. 1873) SWISS
    I/ 100-1200   P/ 100-3400
WUNDERLICH, PAUL (B. 1927) GERMAN
    I/ 100-1200   P/ 25-3900   R/ 230-475
WUSTEN, JOHANNES
    I/ 275-600
WYCK, THOMAS (1616-1677) DUTCH
    I/ 100-450
WYETH, JAMES (B. 1946) AMERICAN
    I/ 500-3300
WYLLIE, WILLIAM LIONEL (1851-1931) BRITISH
    I/ 50-1100
WYNGAERDE, FRANS (1614-1669) FLEMISH
    I/ 690-950
WYNMAN, WIM (B. 1897) DUTCH
    P/ 1700
WYSS, FRANZ ANATOL (?) ?
    I/ 100-550

Technique Key

Under each printing technique you may encounter the following types of prints (or combination of processes):

- **I** Intaglio:
  - etching
  - drypoint
  - steel engraving
  - stipple engraving
  - aquatint
  - mezzotint
  - soft-ground etching
  - crayon manner

- **P** Planographic:
  - lithograph
  - monotype
  - silk-screen
  - cliche verre
  - serigraph

- **R** Relief:
  - wood block
    - woodcut
      - chiaroscuro
    - wood engraving
  - linoleum cut (linocut)

Y

YLEN, JEAN D' (?) ?
P/ 350-1200
YONGHE, JOHN DE (1856-1917) AMERICAN
P/ 300-900
YOSHIDA, HIROSHI (1876-1950) JAPANESE
R/ 100-13000
YOUNG, CHARLES JAC (1880-1940) AMERICAN
I/ 20-100
YOUNGERMAN, JACK (B. 1926) AMERICAN
P/ 75-650
YUNKERS, ADJA (1900-1983) LATVIAN/AMERICAN
P/ 70-1300

Z

ZABOLY, BELA (B. 1910) AMERICAN
I/ 30-90
ZADKINE, OSSIP (1890-1967) RUSSIAN/FRENCH
I/ 30-600   P/ 25-1300   R/ 700
ZAKANITCH, ROBERT (B. 1935) AMERICAN
P/ 200-450
ZANETTI, ANTONIO MARIA (1680-1757) ITALIAN
R/ 150-3300
ZAO-WOU-KI (1921-1964) CHINESE/FRENCH
I/ 125-1450   P/ 100-1100
ZAZINGER, M. (14TH C) GERMAN
I/ 1700
ZEEMAN, REINIER (1623-1667) DUTCH
I/ 100-1800
ZENDER, RUDOLF (20TH C) SWISS
P/ 250-700
ZIEGLER, RICHARD (B. 1901) GERMAN
P/ 500
ZIETARA, WALENTY (?) ?
P/ 200-1500
ZIGLDRUM, FRED A. (?) ?
I/ 150-300

ZILLE, HEINRICH (1858-1929) GERMAN
   I/ 100-2200   P/ 100-6000
ZIMBAL, JOHANN (?) ?
   I/ 500-2600   P/ 194
ZIMMER, HANS PETER (B. 1936) GERMAN
   I/ 75-1900   P/ 465
ZIMMERMANN, MAC (B. 1912) GERMAN
   I/ 50-1200   P/ 50-550
ZINGG, ADRIAN (1934-1816) SWISS
   I/ 150-500
ZOCCHI, GIUSEPPE (1711-1767) ITALIAN
   I/ 560-1950
ZOIR, EMIL (B. 1867) SWEDISH
   I/ 15-50
ZORN, ANDERS (1860-1920) SWEDISH]
   I/ 50-17000
ZUCCARELLI, FRANCESCO (1701-1788) ITALIAN
   I/ 250-1130
ZUCCHI, LORENZO (1704-1779) ITALIAN
   I/ 200
ZUCKER, JOSEPH (B. 1941) AMERICAN
   I/ 100
ZULOW, FRANZ VON (1883-1963) AUSTRIAN
   P/ 50-1900   R/ 1140
ZUNDT, MATTHIAS (1498-1572) GERMAN
   I/ 300-500
ZUNIGA, FRANCISCO (B. 1913) MEXICAN
   P/ 275-3300

Artists in Dealer Catalogs

The following is an alphabetical list of over 425 artists whose prints infrequently turn up at auction, or, prints by these artists appear in "group" lots. (Auction houses will sometimes group together several inexpensive works to make up a sufficient dollar value.) As a result, these lesser-known artists will not have any individual track record at auction and consequently, they will not appear in the main alphabetical section of this guide.

The list emphasizes American, English, and French artists who produced prints primarily from 1860 to 1960. The price range given represents where roughly 75% of an artist's works fall, price wise, based on a broad survey of numerous dealer catalogs.

The printing technique listed (i.e., I, P, or R) is the technique for which he/she is best known. An asterisk (*) after a price range indicates that prints by this artist are rare!

ABBE, SOLOMON VAN (1883-1955) ENGLISH
    I/ 100-200
ABELES, SIGMUND (B. 1934) AMERICAN
    I/ 100-500   P/ 100-500
ABRAMOWITZ, ALBERT (1879-1963) AMERICAN
    R/ 300-400
ADAMS, CLINTON (B. 1918) AMERICAN
    P/ 200-400
ADDAMS, CLIFFORD (1876-1942) AMERICAN
    I/ 100-300
ALDRIN, ANDERS (1889-1970) SWEDISH/AMERICAN
    R/ 300-650
ALPS, GLEN (B. 1914) AMERICAN
    P/ 200-400
ANDERSON, CARLOS (20TH C) AMERICAN
    P/ 100-400
ANDRUS, VERA (1896-1979) AMERICAN
    P/ 200-500
ARNOLD, GRANT (B. 1904) AMERICAN
    P/ 100-300

AUERBACH-LEVY, WILLIAM (1889-1964) AMERICAN
 I/ 150-450
AULT, GEORGE C. (1891-1948) AMERICAN
 P/ 500-1500*   R/ 500-3500*
AUSTIN, ROBERT (1895-1973) BRITISH
 I/ 250-650

B

BACHER, OTTO (1856-1909) AMERICAN
 I 200-600
BAERTSOEN, ALBERT (1866-1922) BELGIAN
 I/ 100-300
BANTING, JOHN (1902-1972) BRITISH
 P/ 500-1000
BARKER, ALBERT (1874-1947) AMERICAN
 P/ 100-600
BARKER, THOMAS (OF BATH) (1769-1847) BRITISH
 P/ 400-700
BARLOW, LOU (B. 1908) AMERICAN
 R/ 100-500
BARRETT, LAWRENCE (B. 1897) AMERICAN
 P/ 100-300
BARTLETT, IVAN (B. 1915) AMERICAN
 R/ 50-150
BASKETT, CHARLES H. (1872-1953) BRITISH
 I/ 100-300
BEAL, GIFFORD (1879-1956) AMERICAN
 I/ 100-300
BECKER, FREDERICK (B. 1913) AMERICAN
 I/ 500-1500
BELL, CECIL C. (1906-1970) AMERICAN
 P/ 200-800
BELLEROCHE, ALBERT (1864-1944) FRENCH
 P/ 500-3000
BENGTZ, TURE (20TH C) AMERICAN
 P/ 100-200
BERMAN, EUGENE (1899-1972) AMERICAN
 P/ 300-600
BIBEL, LEON (B. 1912) AMERICAN

P/ 250-800
BICKNELL, ALBION H. (1837-1915) AMERICAN
P/ 500-2500 (monotypes)
BIELER, ANDRE (B. 1896) SWISS/CANADIAN
R/ 400-800
BLACKBURN, MORRIS (B. 1902) AMERICAN
R/ 400-750
BLACKBURN, ROBERT (B. 1920) AMERICAN
I/ 300-700   P/ 300-700
BLANCH, ARNOLD (1896-1968) AMERICAN
P/ 150-350
BLASHKO, ABE (B. 1920) AMERICAN
P/ 400-900
BLATHERWICK, LILY (1859-1934) BRITISH
P/ 100-300
BLERY, EUGENE (1805-1887) FRENCH
I/ 100-1000
BLOCH, JULIUS (1888-1966) AMERICAN
P/ 150-300
BLOOM, HYMAN (B. 1913) AMERICAN
I/ 500-1000   P/ 500-1500
BLUM, ROBERT F. (1857-1903) AMERICAN
I/ 150-500
BLUMENSCHEIN, HELEN G. (B. 1909) AMERICAN
P/ 150-300
BOCCIONI, UMBERTO (1882-1916) AMERICAN
P/ 150-350
BOONE, CORA (1865-1953) AMERICAN
R/ 300-600
BORMANN, EMMA (B. 1887) GERMAN
R/ 150-350
BOTHWELL, DORR (B. 1902)
P/ 350-750
BOTKE, CORNELIUS (1887-1954) AMERICAN
I/ 200-300   R/ 300-800
BOTKE, JESSIE ARMS (1883-1971) AMERICAN
R/ 500-1500
BOURGEOIS, LOUISE (B. 1911) AMERICAN
I/ 1500-3500*
BOYS, THOMAS SHOTTER (1803-1874) BRITISH
P/ 200-750
BRAUGHT, ROSS (1898-1984) AMERICAN
P/ 200-800
BRODSKY, HARRY (20TH C) AMERICAN

P/ 250-500
BRODZKY, HORACE (1885-1969) BRITISH
    R/ 350-750
BROOK, ALEXANDER (1898-1980) AMERICAN
    P/ 150-250
BROWN, JOHN GEORGE (1831-1913) AMERICAN
    I/ 150-650
BROWN, SYD (B. 1907) AMERICAN
    P/ 100-400
BRUSSEL-SMITH, BERNARD (B. 1914) AMERICAN
    R/ 300-1200
BRY, EDITH (B. 1898) AMERICAN
    P/ 50-200
BUCKLAND-WRIGHT, JOHN (1897-1954) BRITISH
    I/ 150-350
BUFF, CONRAD (1886-1975) AMERICAN
    P/ 2-500
BUMBECK, DAVID (B. 1940) AMERICAN
    I/ 100-500
BURKHARDT, HANS (B. 1904) AMERICAN
    P/ 500-1500*
BUTCHER, ENID (20TH C) BRITISH
    I/ 50-150

C

CALAME, ALEXANDRE (1810-1864) FRENCH
    P/ 50-250
CALAPAI, LETTERIO (B. 1902) AMERICAN
    I/ 500-1500
CALVERT, EDWARD (1799-1883) BRITISH
    R/ 400-1200
CAMERON, KATE (1874-19615) BRITISH
    I/ 100-300
CARROLL, JOHN (1892-1959) AMERICAN
    P/ 100-200
CARTER, FREDERICK (1885-1967) BRITISH
    I/ 50-500
CATLETT, ELIZABETH (B. 1919) AMERICAN
    I/ 300-700

* *Indicates that these prints are rare!*

CHAFFEE, ADA GILMOUR (1883-1955) AMERICAN
R/ 1500-5000*
CHAFFEE, OLIVER NEWBURY JR. (1881-1944) AMERICAN
R/ 750-2000*
CHARPENTIER, ALEXANDRE (1875-1963) FRENCH
P/ 400-850
CHASE, W. CORWIN (1897-1988) AMERICAN
R/ 300-850
CHENEY, PHILIP (B. 1897) AMERICAN
P/ 100-200
CHESNEY, LEE R. (B. 1920) AMERICAN
I/ 200-400
CHEYNE, IAN (1895-1955) SCOTTISH
R/ 350-750
CHURCH, FREDERICK STUART (1842-1924) AMERICAN
I/ 100-300
CLARK, ROLAND (1874-1957) AMERICAN
I/ 200-750
COHN, MAX ARTHUR (B. 1908) AMERICAN
P/ 200-400
COLE, J. FOXCROFT (1837-1892) AMERICAN
I/ 150-300
COLESCOTT, WARRINGTON (20TH C) AMERICAN
P/ 500-1000
COLE, TIMOTHY (1852-1931) AMERICAN
R/ 50-150
COLMAN, SAMUEL (1832-1920) AMERICAN
I/ 100-500
CONSTANT, GEORGE (B. 1892) AMERICAN
I/ 50-250
COPE, CHARLES (1811-1890) BRITISH
I/ 150-300
CSOKA, STEPHEN (1897-1989) HUNGARIAN/AMERICAN
I/ 50-500
COTMAN, JOHN SELL (1782-1842) BRITISH
I/ 250-500
COWERN, RAYMOND (B. 1913) BRITISH
I/ 50-150
CRANE, ALAN (1901-1969) AMERICAN
P/ 100-250
CRESWICK, THOMAS (1811-1869) BRITISH
I/ 150-300
CROME, JOHN (1768-1821) BRITISH
I/ 200-800

D

DAGLISH, ERIC (1894-1966) BRITISH
  R/ 50-150
DAWSON, NELSON (1859-1941) BRITISH
  I/ 100-250
DAY, RICHARD (1896-1972) AMERICAN
  P/ 200-500
DAY, WORDEN (1916-1986) AMERICAN
  R/ 400-1000
DECKER, ALBERT (B. 1919) AMERICAN
  P/ 100-300
DEHAAS, MAURITZ FREDERICK HENDRIK (1832-1895)
  DUTCH/AMERICAN
  I/ 75-250
DEHNER, DOROTHY (B. 1901) AMERICAN
  I/ 400-800
DESMAZIERES, ERIK (B. 1948) FRENCH
  I/ 500-1500
DEVERIA, ACHILLE (1800-1857) FRENCH
  P/ 200-500
DEWOLF, WALLACE (1854-1930) AMERICAN
  I/ 50-150
DIELMAN, FREDERICK (1847-1935) AMERICAN
  I/ 50-300
DOI, ISAMI (1903-1965) AMERICAN
  R/ 350-1200
DUPONT, PIETER (1870-1911) DUTCH
  I/ 100-400
DUPRE, JULES (1811-1889) FRENCH
  P/ 100-400
DURAND, ASHER (1796-1886) AMERICAN
  I/ 500-3500*
DURLEUX, CAROLINE (B. 1896) AMERICAN
  P/ 100-600

E

*   *Indicates that these prints are rare!*

EDMONDSON, LEONARD (B. 1916) AMERICAN
I/ 300-750
EXLEY, J.R.G. (1878-1967) BRITISH
I/ 100-450

F

FABRI, RALPH (1894-1975) AMERICAN
I/ 200-400
FALCONER, JOHN M. (1820-1903) AMERICAN
I/ 50-200
FALILEEF, VADIM DMITRI (1879-1948) RUSSIAN
R/ 300-750
FARRER, HENRY (1843-1903) AMERICAN
I/ 50-400
FAY, CLARK (1894-1956) AMERICAN
I/ 200-750
FEITELSON, LORSER (1898-1978) AMERICAN
P/ 500-1200*
FERREN, JOHN (1905-1970) AMERICAN
I/ 500-1000*   R/ 500-1500*
FIGURA, HANS (B. 1898) AUSTRIAN
I/ 100-300
FITSCH, EUGENE C. (1892-1972) AMERICAN
P/ 300-700
FISKE, GERTRUDE (1879-1961) AMERICAN
I/ 200-500
FITTON, HEDLEY (1859-1929) BRITISH
I/ 50-250
FLOETHE, RICHARD (1901-1988) AMERICAN
P/ 200-400
FOOKES, URSULA (active 1920-1930) BRITISH
R/ 300-600
FRANK, LEO (B. 1884) AUSTGRIAN
R/ 200-350
FREED, ERNEST (20TH C) AMERICAN
I/ 1000-3000
FULLER, SUE (B. 1914) AMERICAN
I/ 200-600
FULWIDER, EDWIN (20TH C) AMERICAN

P/ 100-500

G

GANDARA, ANTONIO DE LA (1862-1917) FRENCH
P/ 300-600
GASKELL, PERCIVAL (1868-1934) BRITISH
I/ 100-300
GEARHART, MAY (1872-1951) AMERICAN
I/ 200-500
GELLER, TODROS (1889-1949) AMERICAN
R/ 200-500
GELLERT, HUGO (B. 1892) HUNGARIAN/AMERICAN
P/ 250-850
GIBBINGS, ROBERT (1889-1958) BRITISH
R/ 50-400
GIFFORD, ROBERT SWAIN (1840-1905) AMERICAN
I/ 100-500
GILES, WILLIAM (1872-1939) BRITISH
I/ 500-1000   R/ 500-1000
GLINTENKAMP, HENRY (1887-1946) AMERICAN
R/ 100-300
GOODEN, STEPHEN (B. 1892) BRITISH
I/ 100-300
GOSSE, SYLVIA (1881-1968) BRITISH
I/ 250-400
GOTTLIEB, HARRY (1894-1992) AMERICAN
I/ 50-250   P/ 200-700
GREAVES, WALTER (1846-1930) BRITISH
I/ 200-400
GREENGRASS, WILLIAM E. (1896-1970) BRITISH
R/ 800-2500
GREENWOOD, MARION (1909-1970) AMERICAN
P/ 100-800
GROSS, ANTHONY (1905-1984) BRITISH
I/ 300-1500
GROSS-BETTELHEIM, JOLAN (B. 1900) AMERICAN
I/ 500-3000   P/ 1000-10000*

* *Indicates that these prints are rare!*

H

HAGEDORN, EDWARD (1902-1982) AMERICAN
I/ 200-1200
HALL, NORMA BASSETT (1889-1957) AMERICAN
R/ 400-800
HALL, OLIVER (1869-1957) BRITISH
I/ 100-200
HANDFORTH, THOMAS (1897-1948) AMERICAN
I/ 50-150
HARARI, HANANIAH (B. 1912) AMERICAN
P/ 400-2000
HARDIE, MARTIN (1875-1952) BRITISH
I/ 50-250
HARKER, KATHARINE VAN DYKE (1872-1966) AMERICAN
R/ 300-600
HAUPERS, CLEMENT (B. 1900) AMERICAN
I/ 100-400
HAVENS, JAMES D. (B. 1900) AMERICAN
R/ 150-350
HAY, JAMES HAMILTON (1874-1916) BRITISH
I/ 50-200
HAZEN, BESSIE ELLA (1861-1946) AMERICAN
R/ 100-300
HECKMAN, ALBERT (1893-1971) AMERICAN
I/ 150-500   P/ 200-500
HEINS, JOHN (1896-1960) AMERICAN
P/ 100-300
HELLER, HELEN WEST (1872-1955) AMERICAN
R/ 200-800
HENDERSON, LESLIE (B. 1895) AMERICAN
I/ 75-250
HERVIER, ADOLPHE (1821-1879) FRENCH
I/ 100-500
HEYMAN, CHARLES (1881-1915) BRITISH
I/ 100-250
HIGGINS, EUGENE (1874-1958) AMERICAN
I/ 50-250
HNIZDOVSKY, JACQUES (1915-1985) AMERICAN
R/ 50-400
HOBART, CLARK (1868-1948) AMERICAN
P/ 300-600
HOOK, JAMES (1819-1907) BRITISH

I/ 100-300
HOWARTH, ALBANY E. (1872-1936) BRITISH
   I/ 50-150
HUGO, IAN (1900-1984) AMERICAN
   I/ 400-800
HUNT, WILLIAM HOLMAN (1827-1910) BRITISH
   I/ 250-800
HUNT, WILLIAM MORRIS (1824-1879) AMERICAN
   P/ 1000-3000
HUTCHINSON, LEONARD (1896-1980) CANADIAN
   R/ 100-300
HUTTY, ALFRED (1877-1954) AMERICAN
   I/ 200-450

J

JACOBI, ELI (1898-1984) AMERICAN
   R/ 100-800
JACQUEMART, JULES (1837-1880) FRENCH
   I/ 100-600
JANES, NORMAN (B. 1892) BRITISH
   I/ 50-200
JOHNSON, SARGENT CLAUDE (1888-1967) AMERICAN
   P/ 1000-2500*
JOHNSTON, DAVID CLAYPOOL (1797-1865) AMERICAN
   I/ 300-500
JO MESS, GEORGE (1898-1962) AMERICAN
   I/ 100-400
JUDSON, JANE BERRY (20TH C) AMERICAN
   R/ 200-400
JULES, MERVIN (B. 1912) AMERICAN
   P/ 100-400   R/ 75-150

K

KEENE, CHARLES (1823-1891) BRITISH
I/ 100-350
KELLY, JOHN MELVILLE (B. 1879) AMERICAN
P/ 100-400
KENT, NORMAN (1903-1972) AMERICAN
R/ 50-150
KINNEY, TROY (1871-1938) AMERICAN
I/ 50-200
KIPNISS, ROBERT (B. 1931) AMERICAN
P/ 200-600
KNATHS, KARL (1891-1971) AMERICAN
P/ 250-500   R/ 1000-1800
KNIGHT, CLAYTON (B. 1891) AMERICAN
P/ 100-250
KOMJATI, JULIUS (1894-1958) HUNGARIAN
I/ 50-250
KOSA, EMIL JR. (1903-1968)
I 500-800
KOVNER, SAUL (B. 1904) AMERICAN
P/ 150-500
KRASNOW, PETER (1887-1980) AMERICAN
P/ 400-1000
KUPFERMAN, LAWRENCE (B. 1909) AMERICAN
I/ 250-1500

L

LACY, LUCILE LAND (B. 1901) AMERICAN
P/ 100-400
LAMORE,CHET (1908-1980) AMERICAN
P 200-700
LANDON, EDWARD (1911-1984) AMERICAN
P/ 300-700
LANFAIR, HARRIET KEESE (B. 1900) AMERICAN
P/ 100-200
LANKES, JULIUS J. (1884-1960) AMERICAN
R/ 75-250
LARKINS, WILLIAM (1901-1974) BRITISH
I/ 50-300
LATHROP, DOROTHY (B. 1891) AMERICAN

P/ 500-200
LEAR, EDWARD (1812-1888) BRITISH
P/ 100-450
LEE, DORIS (1905-1983) AMERICAN
P/ 100-300
LEE, SYDNEY (1866-1949) BRITISH
I/ 50-250
LEIGH, WILLIAM R. (1866-1955) AMERICAN
I/ 2000-4000*
LEITHAUSER, MARK (B. 1950) AMERICAN
I/ 500-1000
LINDSAY, LIONEL (1874-1961) AUSTRALIAN
R/ 100-400
LITTEN, SIDNEY M. (1887-1949) BRITISH
I/ 50-250
LOCKYEAR, ISABEL DE (1895-1980) BRITISH
R/ 250-450
LOGAN, ROBERT (B. 1890) AMERICAN
I/ 50-200
LOGGIE, HELEN A. (D. 1976) AMERICAN
I/ 50-100
LOVET-LORSKI, BORIS (1894-1973) LITHUANIAN-AMERICAN
P/ 400-800
LOWELL, NAT (B. 1880) AMERICAN
I/ 100-400
LOWENGRUND, MARGARET (1905-1957) AMERICAN
P/ 200-500
LUCAS, DAVID (1802-1881) BRITISH
I/ 150-1500
LUNDBERG, HELEN (B. 1908) AMERICAN
P/ 300-1000

M

MACBETH-RAEBURN, HENRY (1869-1947) BRITISH
I/ 50-200
MACLAUGHLAN, DONALD SHAW (1876-1938) CANADIAN/AMERICAN
I/ 100-250
MACLEOD, WILLIAM DOUGLAS (1892-1963) BRITISH
I/ 50-200

MACNAB, IAIN (1890-1967) BRITISH
R/ 50-300
MAGAFAN, ETHEL (B. 1916) AMERICAN
P/ 100-400
MAGAFAN, JENNE (1916-1952) AMERICAN
P/ 100-400
MALET, GUY (1900-1973) BRITISH
R/ 50-200
MANDELMAN, BEATRICE (B. 1912) AMERICAN
P/ 200-500
MARGO, BORIS (B 1902) AMERICAN
R/ 800-1500
MARTIN, FLETCHER (1904-1979) AMERICAN
P/ 300-1500
MASON, ALICE TRUMBULL (1904-1971) AMERICAN
I/ 1000-2000
MAZUR, MICHAEL (B. 1935) AMERICAN
I/ 300-1500   P/ 300-3000
MCCLELLAN, JOHN (1808-1886) AMERICAN
P/ 200-500
MCCLUNG, FLORENCE (1894-1992) AMERICAN
P 300-700
MCCRADY, JOHN (1911-1968) AMERICAN
P/ 200-700
MCCRAY, DOROTHY (20TH C) AMERICAN
I/ 500-1500
MCVEIGH, BLANCHE (1896-1970) AMERICAN
I/ 150-400
MCVICKER, JAY (B. 1911) AMERICAN
I/ 300-700
MEAD, RODERICK (B. 1900) AMERICAN
R/ 100-400
MEERT, JOSEPH (1905-1990) AMERICAN
P/ 200-500
MEESER, LILIAN (1864-1942) AMERICAN
R/ 500-1200
MEISSNER, LEO (B. 1895) AMERICAN
R/ 50-500
MEISSONIER, JEAN LOUIS ERNEST (1815-1891) FRENCH
I/ 100-500
MENIHAN, JOHN (B. 1908) AMERICAN
I/ 150-500
MERSHIMER, FREDERICK (B. 1958) AMERICAN
I/ 150-500

MESQUITA, SAMUEL DE (1868-1944) DUTCH
    I/ 400-800
MESSENGER, IVAN (1895-1983) AMERICAN
    P/ 150-300
MESSIBOV, HUGH (B.1916) AMERICAN
    I 500-1500
MEYEROWITZ, WILLIAM (B. 1908) AMERICAN
    I/ 250-750
MIELATZ, CHARLES FREDERICK (1864-1919) AMERICAN
    I/ 200-600
MILLER, LILLIAM MAY (1895-1945) AMERICAN
    R/ 100-300
MONKS, JOHN AUSTIN (1850-1917) AMERICAN
    I/ 75-250
MORAN, MARY NIMMO (1842-1899) AMERICAN
    I/ 150-750
MORGAN, WILLIAM E.C. (B. 1903) BRITISH
    I/ 100-300
MORTIMER, JOHN HAMILTON (1740-1779) BRITISH
    I/ 200-500
MORTON, CONCORD AND CAVENDISH (B. 1911) BRITISH
    R/ 250-500
MOY, SEONG (B. 1921) AMERICAN
    R/ 500-2000
MUENCH, JOHN (B. 1914) AMERICAN
    P/ 300-500   R/ 300-500
MULLINEUX, MARY (1875-1965) AMERICAN
    R/ 800-2500*
MURPHY, JOHN J.A. (1888-1967) AMERICAN
    R/ 1000-3500
MYERS, JEROME (1867-1940) AMERICAN
    I/ 100-500

N

NAGLER, FRED (B. 1891) AMERICAN
    I/ 50-100
NANKIVELL, FRANK (B. 1869) AMERICAN
    I/ 100-300
NANTEUIL, CELESTIN (1813-1873) FRENCH

I/ 100-400
NICHOLL, JAMES C. (1847-1918) AMERICAN
   I/ 50-200
NIXON, JOB (1891-1938) ENGLISH
   I/ 100-300
NORTON, ELIZABETH (B. 1887) AMERICAN
   R/ 200-500

O

OGILVIE, HELEN (B. 1902) AUSTRALIAN
   R/ 100-250
OLDS, ELIZABETH (B. 1896) AMERICAN
   P/ 500-1000
O'NEILL, GEORGE BERNARD (1828-1917) BRITISH
   I/ 50-200
ORR, LOUIS (1879-1961) AMERICAN
   I/ 150-600
OSBORNE, MALCOLM (B. 1880) BRITISH
   I/ 50-300

P

PACKARD, EMMY LOU (B. 1914) AMERICAN
   R/ 400-800
PAXTON, WILLIAM (1869-1941) AMERICAN
   I/ 400-1200
PEAVY, PAULINA (B. 1901) AMERICAN
   R/ 100-200
PECK, EDIKTH HOGEN (B. 1884) AMERICAN
   I/ 100-250
PETERS, ROBERT C. (B. 1888) BRITISH
   I/ 100-250
PETERSEN, MARTIN (1866-1956) AMERICAN
   I/ 150-600
PICKHARDT, CARL (B. 1908) AMERICAN

P/ 150-450
PINTO, ANGELO (B. 1908) AMERICAN
    R/ 150-600
PINTO, SALVATORE (1905-1966) AMERICAN
    R/ 150-600
PITTMAN, HOBSON (1900-1972) AMERICAN
    R/ 200-300
PLATT, CHARLES ADAMS (1861-1933) AMERICAN
    I/ 150-500
PLEISSNER, OGDEN M. (1905-1983) AMERICAN
    I/ 750-1500
POND, CLAYTON (B. 1941) AMERICAN
    I/ 100-300
PREISSIG, VOJTECH (1873-1944) CZECHOSLOVAKIAN
    I/ 200-400
PROUVE, VICTOR (1853-1943) FRENCH
    I/ 200-800
PULSIFER, MINA (B. 1899) AMERICAN
    P/ 200-400
PYTLACK, LEONARD (B. 1910) AMERICAN
    P/ 300-2000   R/ 400-800

Q

QUEST, CHARLES F.(B. 1904) AMERICAN
    R/ 400-1000

R

RACKLEY, MILDRED (1906-1992) AMERICAN
    P/ 400-800   R/ 100-400
RAFFET, AUGUSTE (1804-1860) FRENCH
    P/ 100-500
RATHBONE, AUGUSTA (B. 1897) AMERICAN
    I/ 200-500
REED, DOEL (B. 1894) AMERICAN

I/ 500-2000
REIN, HARRY (B. 1914) AMERICAN
P/ 200-400
REISMAN, PHILLIP (1904-1992) AMERICAN
I/ 150-400
RENOUARD, PAUL (1845-1924) FRENCH
I/ 200-500
RICE, WILLIAM S. (1873-1963) AMERICAN
R/ 300-750
RICKETTS, CHARLES (1866-1931) BRITISH
R/ 100-400
RIST, LUIGI (1888-1959) AMERICAN
R/ 1500-5000
ROBERTSON, DAVID (B. 1885) BRITISH
I/ 50-200
ROBERTSON, PERCY (1869-1934) ENGLISH
I/ 50-200
ROBINS, WILLIAM P. (1882-1959) BRITISH
I/ 50-250
ROBINSON, BOARDMAN (1876-1952) AMERICAN
P/ 100-400
ROGALSKI, WALTER (B. 1925) AMERICAN
I/ 100-400
ROSE, RUTH STARR (1887-1965) AMERICAN
P/ 200-400
ROSENBERG, JAMES N. (1874-1970) AMERICAN
P/ 400-800
ROYDS, MABEL A. (1874-1941) BRITISH
R/ 200-600
RUBENSTEIN, LEWIS (B. 1908) AMERICAN
P/ 300-900
RUELLAN, ANDREE (B. 1905) AMERICAN
P/ 100-250
RUSHBURY, SIR HENRY (1880-1968) BRITISH
I/ 100-250
RUSSELL, SHIRLEY (B. 1886) AMERICAN
R/ 150-350
RUZICKA, RUDOLPH (1883-1962) AMERICAN
R/ 100-400

S

SALEMME, LUCIA (B. 1919) AMERICAN
 R/ 250-450
SANDBY, PAUL (1730-1809) BRITISH
 I/ 100-750
SANDZEN, BIRGER (1871-1954) SWEDISH/AMERICAN
 R/ 150-450
SARGENT, JOHN SINGER (1856-1925) AMERICAN
 P/ 7500-20000*
SCHALDACH, WILLIAM (B. 1896) AMERICAN
 I/ 150-400
SCHILLING, ALEXANDER (1859-1937) AMERICAN
 I/ 100-300
SCHOPPE, PALMER (B. 1912) AMERICAN
 P/ 300-750
SCHREIBER, GEORGE (B. 1904) AMERICAN
 P/ 100-300
SCHWARTZ, WILLIAM S. (1896-1933) AMERICAN
 P/ 400-1200
SCOTT, STANLEY (20TH C) AMERICAN
 R/ 150-350
SEABY, ALLEN (1867-1953) BRITISH
 R/ 400-800
SENSENEY, GEORGE (1874-1943) AMERICAN
 I/ 300-750
SHARP, WILLIAM (1803-1875) AMERICAN
 P/ 100-2000
SHARP, WILLIAM (1900-1961) AMERICAN
 I/ 200-400
SHERMAN, RUSSELL (20TH C) AMERICAN
 P/ 50-200
SHORE, HENRIETTE (1880-1963) AMERICAN
 P/ 300-500
SHUSTER, WILL (1893-1969) AMERICAN
 I/ 100-300
SIMPSON, JOSEPH (1879-1939) BRITISH
 I/ 100-200
SLATER, ERIC (B. 1896) ENGLISH
 R/ 200-500
SLOAN, HELEN FARR (20THC) AMERICAN
 P 200-700
SMART, DOUGLAS IAN (1879-1970) BRITISH

I/ 50-200
SMITH, DAVID (B. 1906) AMERICAN
    P/ 1500-10000*
SMITH, PERCY (1882-1948) BRITISH
    I/ 50-300
SMITH, WUANITA (1866-1959) AMERICAN
    R/ 500-1500
SOPER, EILEEN A. (1905-1990) ENGLISH
    I/ 100-250
SPARKS, NATHANIEL (1880-1957) BRITISH
    I/ 100-250
SPENCER, NILES (1893-1952) AMERICAN
    P/ 5000-15000*
STAVENITZ, ALEXANDER (1901-1960) AMERICAN
    I/ 100-400
STEFFEN, BERNARD (1907-1980) AMERICAN
    P/ 500-1500
STORRS, JOHN (1885-1956) AMERICAN
    R/ 500-3500*
STRANG, IAN (B. 1886) SCOTTISH
    I/ 100-400
SURENDORF, CHARLES (B. 1906) AMERICAN
    R/ 100-300
SWANN, JAMES (1905-1985) AMERICAN
    I/ 100-500
SZANTO, LOUIS (1889-1965) AMERICAN
    I/ 50-200

T

TAKAL, PETER (B. 1905) AMERICAN
    I/ 300-750
TANNER, ROBIN (B. 1904) BRITISH
    I/ 500-1500
TAYLOR, CHARLES WILLIAM (1878-1960) BRITISH
    I/ 50-150
TAYLOR, GRACE MARTIN (B. 1903) AMERICAN
    R/ 1000-2500*
THRASH, DOX (B. 1892) AMERICAN
    I/ 200-400

TROY, ADRIAN (B. 1901) AMERICAN
R/ 100-250
TUBIS, SEYMOUR (B. 1919) AMERICAN
I/ 200-500
TURNBULL, JAMES (1907-1977) AMERICAN
P/ 300-600
TURZAK, CHARLES (1899-1986) AMERICAN
R/ 200-1800
TUSHINGHAM, SIDNEY (1884-1968) BRITISH
I/ 100-300

U

UCHIMA, ANSEI (B. 1921) AMERICAN
R/ 400-900
UNDERWOOD, LEON (1890-1975) ENGLISH
R/ 100-1000
UNWIN, NORA (1907-1982) AMERICAN
R/ 50-250
URBAN, ALBERT (B. 1911) AMERICAN
P/ 500-1500

V

VALERIO, ALESSANDRO MASTRO (1887-1953) AMERICAN
I/ 200-400
VAN ELTEN, KRUSEMAN (1829-1904) DUTCH/AMERICAN
I/ 50-200
VAN VLIET, CLAIRE (B. 1933) CANADIAN-AMERICAN
P/ 100-250
VELONIS, ANTHONY (B. 1911) AMERICAN
P/ 150-1500
VOGEL, DONALD (B. 1917) AMERICAN
I/ 200-600
VOGEL, JOSEPH (B. 1911) AMERICAN
P/ 1000-2000

VONDROUS, JAN C. (B. 1884) CZECH
I/ 50-250
VON NEUMANN, ROBERT (B. 1888) AMERICAN
P/ 50-150
VONWICHT, JOHN (1888-1970) AMERICAN
P/ 400-1500

W

WACKERNAGEL, OTTO (B. 1885) AMERICAN
I/ 50-150
WALD, SYLVIA (B. 1915) AMERICAN
P/ 1500-4000
WALES, GEORGE C. (1868-1940) AMERICAN
I/ 50-250   P/ 100-300
WARD, JAMES (1769-1859) BRITISH
P/ 500-1500
WARD, LYND (1905-1985) AMERICAN
R/ 50-250
WARING, LAURA WHEELER (1877-1948) AMERICAN
R/ 100-300
WARLOW, HERBERT GORDON (1885-1942) BRITISH
I/ 50-150
WARSAGER, HYMAN (1909-1974) AMERICAN
P/ 150-300
WARTHEN, FEROL (1890-1987) AMERICAN
R/ 750-2500*
WASHBURN, CADWALLADER (1866-1965) AMERICAN
I/ 50-250
WATERS, HERBERT (B. 1903) AMERICAN
R/ 50-200
WAY, THOMAS (1862-1913) BRITISH
P/ 100-350
WAYNE, JUNE (B. 1918) AMERICAN
P/ 500-2500
WEIDENAAR, REYNOLD (1915-1985) AMERICAN
I/ 500-2500
WENDELL, THEODORE (1859-1932) AMERICAN
I/ 200-500
WEIR, J. ALDEN (1852-1919) AMERICAN

I/ 500-2000*
WHEETE, GLENN (B. 1884) AMERICAN
  R/ 100-300
WHITE, THEO (1902-1978) AMERICAN
  P/ 100-400
WHYDALE, ERNEST HERBERT (1886-1952) BRITISH
  I/ 50-200
WICKEY, HARRY (B. 1892) AMERICAN
  I/ 300-500
WILBUR, LAWRENCE (B. 1897) AMERICAN
  I/ 400-1500   R/ 200-400
WILKIE, SIR DAVID (1785-1841) BRITISH
  I/ 100-400
WILKINS, GLADYS M. (B. 1907) AMERICAN
  R/ 75-200
WILKINSON, NORMAN (1878-1971) BRITISH
  I/ 50-200
WILSON, CHARLES BANKS (B. 1918) AMERICAN
  P/ 150-450
WILZENREID, HENRY E. (B. 1892) AMERICAN
  P/ 100-250   R/ 100-250
WOICESKE, RONAU (1887-1953) AMERICAN
  I/ 100-200
WOOD, THOMAS WATERMAN (1823-1903) AMERICAN
  I/ 250-1500
WRIGHT, JOHN BUCKLAND (1897-1954) BRITISH
  I/ 100-400

Z

ZORACH, MARGUERITE (1887-1968) AMERICAN
  R/ 500-2500*
ZORACH, WILLIAM (1887-1966) AMERICAN
  R/ 1000-3500*
ZSISSLY, MALVIN MARR ALBRIGHT (B. 1897) AMERICAN
  P/ 100-250

Technique Key

Under each <u>printing technique</u> you may encounter the following types of prints (or combination of processes):

- **I** <u>Intaglio:</u>
    - etching
    - drypoint
    - steel engraving
    - stipple engraving
    - aquatint
    - mezzotint
    - soft-ground etching
    - crayon manner

- **P** <u>Planographic:</u>
    - lithograph
    - monotype
    - silk-screen
    - cliche verre
    - serigraph

- **R** <u>Relief:</u>
    - wood block
        - woodcut
            - chiaroscuro
        - wood engraving
    - linoleum cut (linocut)

APPENDIX

BIBLIOGRAPHY

AMERICAN PRINTS

Acton, David. *A Spectrum of Innovation; Color in American Printmaking 1890-1960.* New York: W.W. Norton & Co., 1990

Adams, Clinton. *American Lithographers, Nineteen Hundred to Nineteen Sixty: The Artists & Their Printers.* Apollo.

Art & Commerce: American Prints of the Nineteenth Century. University Press of Virginia, 1978.

Bruhn, Thomas P.. *American Etchings: The 1880's.* Storrs, Connecticut: Benton, Museum of Art, 1985

Carey, Francis and Griffiths, Anthony. *American Prints 1879-1979.* London, The British Museum, 1980

Dolmetsch, Joan D. *Eighteenth-Century Prints in Colonial America: To Educate & Decorate.* University Press of Virginia, 1979.

Falk, Peter Hastings. *Who Was Who in American Art.* Sound View Press, 1985

Feinblatt, Ebria and Davis, Bruce. *Los Angeles Prints 1883-1980.* Los Angeles : Los Angeles County Museum of Art, 1980

Field, Richard S. et al. *American Prints 1900-1950.* New Haven : Yale University Art Gallery, 1983.

Fielding, Mantle. *American Engravers upon Copper & Steel.* B. Franklin, 1964. Reproduction of 1917 edition.

Flint, Janet. *Provincetown Printers: A Woodcut Tradition.* Washington: Smithsonian Institution Press, 1983.

Fowble, E. McSherry. *Two Centuries of Prints in America, 1680-1880:*

A Selective Catalogue of the Winterthur Collection. University Press of Virginia, 1988.

Getscher, Robert H. and Staley, Allen. *The Stamp of Whistler*. Oberlin, Ohio: Allen Memorial Art Museum, 1977

Hitchings, Sinclair; Lewis, R.E.; Vershbow, Arthur. *Print Collecting Today*—A Symposium. Boston: Boston Public Library, 1969.

Jacobowitz, Ellen S. and Marcus, George. *American Graphics 1860 - 1940*. Philadelphia; Philadelphia Museum of Art, 1982.

Johnson, Deborah J., and Urbanelli, Lora S. *American Prints Eighteen Seventy to Nineteen Fifty: Whistler to Weidenaar*. Museum of Art Rhode Island, 1987.

Johnson, Una. *American Prints and Printmakers*. Garden City, New York: Doubleday & Co., 1980.

Kraeft, June and Norman. *Great American Prints 1900-1950*. New York: Dover Publications, 1984

Munsing, Stephanie A., ed. *Made in America: Printmaking, 1760-1860)*. Library Co. Philadelphia, 1973.

Museum of Graphic Art. *American Printmaking: The First 150 Years*. Washington, D.C.: Smithsonian Institution Press, 1972.

Museum of Mordern Art, New York, *American Prints 1960-1985*, In The Collection of the Museum of Modern Art; Princeton New Jersey, Princeton University Press, 1986

O'Gorman, James F., ed. *Aspects of American Printmaking, 1800-1950*. Syracuse University Press, 1988

Reaves, Wendy Wick, ed. *American Portrait Prints*. Charlottesville: University of Virginia Press, 1984.

Reese, Albert. *American Prize Prints of the 20th Century*. New York: American Artists Group, 1949.

Reps, John W. *Cities on Stone: Nineteenth Century Lithograph Images of the Urban West*. Univ. of Texas Press: Amon Carter, 1976.

Tatham, David, ed. *Prints & Printmakers of New York State, 1825-1940*. Syracuse University Press, 1986.

Tyler, Francine. *American Etchings of the Ninteenth Century*, New York : Dover Publications, 1984

Tyler, Ron, ed. *Prints of the American West*. Fort Worth: Amon Carter Museum 1983.

Watrous, James. *A Century of American Printmaking, 1880- 1980*. University of Wisconsin Press, 1984.

Whitehill, Walter M., and Hitchings, Sinclair H., eds. *Boston Prints & Printmakers, Sixteen Seventy to Seventeen Seventy-Five*. Published by Colonial Society MA. University Press of Virginia, 1973.

Williams, Reba and Dave. *American Screenprints*. New York: National Academy of Design, 1987.

Wilson, Raymond L. *Index of American Print Exhibitions, 1882-1940*. Scarecrow, 1988.

Young, W. *Dictionary of American Artists, Sculptors & Engravers*. Apollo.

GENERAL

American Lithographers 1900-1960: The Artists & Their Printers. Univ. of New Mexico Press, 1987.

Baas, Jacquelynn and Field, Richard S. *The Artistic Revival of the Woodcut in France 1850-1900*. Ann Arbor: University of Michigan, 1984

Bridgewater, Alan & Bridgewater, Gill. *Printing with Wood Blocks, Stencils & Engravings*. Arco, 1983.

Buckland-Wright, John *Etching & Engraving*. Dover, 1973.

Carlson, Victor and Ittlmann, John. *Regency to Empire, French Printmaking 1715-1814*. Minneapolis: Minneapolis Institute of Arts, 1984

Carey, Francis and Griffiths, Anthony. *From Manet to Toulouse-Lautrec*. London: British Museum, 1978

Carey, Francis and Griffiths, Anthony. *The Print in Germany 1880-1933*. New York: Harper and Row. 1984.

Chamberlain, Walter. *The Thames & Hudson Manual of Etching & Engraving.* Thames Hudson, 1978.

Cleaver, James. *History of Graphic Art.* Greenwood, 1963.

Buchwald, Emilie, ed. *One-of-a-Kind Monoprints: A Creative Process.* Forecast Pap., 1984.

Dyson, Anthony. *Pictures to Print: The Nineteenth- Century Engraving Trade.* Book Press Ltd., 1985.

Eichenberg, Fritz. *The Art of the Print.* New York: Abrams, 1976

Getlein, Frank and Dorothy. *The Bite of the Print.* New York: Clarkson N. Potter, 1963.

Gilmour, Pat. *Modern Prints.* London: Studio Vista, 1970.

Gingold, Diane J., ed. *Master Prints from the Fifteenth Through Eighteenth Centuries.* Montgomery Museum, 1977.

Godfrey, Richard T. *Printmaking in Britain.* New York: New York University Press, 1978.

Guichard, Kenneth. *British Etchers 1850-1940.* london: Robin Gaston, 1983

Haab, Armin. *Mexican Graphic Art.* English edition. Switzerland: C.C. Palmer, 1957.

Harper, J. Russell. *Early Painters & Engravers in Canada.* Apollo, 1981.

Hayter, Stanley William. *About Prints.* London: Oxford University Press, 1962.

Heller, Reinhold, et. al., *Brucke, German Expressionist Prints from the Granvil and Marcia Specks Collection.* Evanston: Northwestern University, 1988.

Hind, Arthur M. *History of Engraving & Etching: From the Fifteenth Century to the Year 1914.* Dover, 1923.

Hind, Arthur M. *A History of Engraving and Etching.* London and New York, 1935. Reprint. New York: Dover Publications, 1963.

Ives, Colta Feller. *The Great Wave: The Influence of Japanese Woodcuts on French Prints.* New York: Metropolitan Museum of Art, 1974.

Ivins, William M., Jr. *Notes on Prints.* Cambridge: M.I.T. Press, 1967.

Ivins, William M., Jr. *Prints & Books.* Da Capo, 1969.

Johnson, Diane and Schrader, J.L. *1450-1550: The Golden Age of Woodcut. The Woodcut Revival 1800-1925.* Lawrence, Kan.: University of Kansas Museum of Art, 1968.

Johnson, Una E. *Ambrose Vollard, Editeur.* New York: Museum of Mordern Art, 1977

Karpinski, Caroline. *Italian Printmaking, Fifteenth & Sixteenth Centures: An Annotated Bibliography.* G.K. Hall, 1987.

Lieberman, William S. "Prints" in *German Art of the Twentieth Century.* New York: Museum of Modern Art, 1957.

Ludman, Joan, and Mason, Lauris. *Fine Print References: A Selected Bibliography of Print-Related Literature.* Sirefman, Carol, ed.: Kraus International, 1982.

Man, Felix H. *Artists' Lithographs.* New York: G.P. Putnam's Sons, 1970.

Mason, Lauris, & Ludman, Joan, eds. *Print Collector's Quarterly: An Anthology of Essays on Eminent Printmakers of the World, 10 Volumes.* Kraus International, 1977.

Masterworks in Wood: The Woodcut Print, from the 15th to the Early 20th Century. Published by Portland Art Museum: University of Washington Press, 1976.

Mayor, A. Hyatt. *The Metropolitan Museum Guide to the Collections-Prints.* New York: Metropolitan Museum of Art, 1964.

Museum of Modern Art. *The Abby Aldrich Rockefeller Print Room.* New York, 1949. New York, 1958.

Opitz, Glenn B. *Mantle Fieldings Dictionary of American Painters, Sculptors, and Engravers.* 2nd revised edition. Apollo, 1986

The Painterly Print; Monotypes from the Seventeenth to the Twentieth Century. New York: Metropolitan Museum of Art, 1980.

Passeron, Roger. *French Prints of the 20th Century.* New York: Praeger, 1970.

Peterdi, Gabor. *Great Prints of the World.* New York: Macmillan, 1969.

Print Reference Sources: A Selected Bibliography, 18th- 20th Centuries. 2nd edition: Kraus International, 1979.

Reed, Sue W. and Wallace, Richard. *Italian Etchers of the Renaissance and Baroque.* Boston: Museum of Fine Arts, 1989

Ross, John & Romano, Clare. *The Complete Intaglio Print.* Free Press, 1974.

Ross, John & Romano, Clare. *The Complete Screen Print & the Lithograph.* Free Press, 1974.

Sachs, Paul J. *Modern Prints and Drawings.* New York: Alfred A. Knopf, 1954.

Sheppard's International Directory of Print & Map Dealers. Published by Europa Publications Ltd., England. Seven Hills Books, 1987.

Shikes, Ralph e. *The Indignant Eye.* Boston: Beacon Press, 1969

Stubbe, Wolf. *Graphic Arts in the Twentieth Century.* New York: Praeger, 1963.

Urbanelli, Lora. *The Grosvenor School, British Linocuts Between the Wars.* Providence: Rhode Island School of Design, 1988

Weber, Wilhelm. *A History of Lithography.* London, Thames & Hudson, 1966.

Wechsler, Herman J. *Great Prints & Printmakers.* New York: Harry N. Abrams, 1967.

Weisberg, Gabriel P. *Social Concern and the Worker: French Prints from 1830-1910.* Salt Lake City: Utah Museum of Fine Arts, 1974.

Wilder, F. L. *How to Identify Old Prints.* London: G. Bell and Sons, 1969.

Zigrosser, Carl. *The Appeal of Prints.* Philadelphia: Leary's Book Co., 1970.

Zigrosser, Carl. *Prints and Their Creators, A World History.* New York: Crown Publishers, 1974.

CONTEMPORARY PRINTS

Ackley, Clifford S. *70's into 80's: Printmaking Now*. Boston: Museum of Fine Arts, 1987

Baro, Gene. *30 Years of American Printmaking*. New York: Brooklyn Museum, 1977

Bloch, E. Maurice. *Tamarind; A Renaissance of Lithography*. International Exhibitions Foundation, 1972

Castleman, Riva. *American Impressions: Prints Since Pollock*. New York: Knopf, 1985

Castleman, Riva. *Contemporary Prints*. New York: Viking Press, 1973.

Castleman, Riva. *Prints of the Twentieth Century*. London, Thames & Hudson, 1976

Field, Richard S., and Fine, Ruth E. *A Graphic Muse: Prints by Contemporary American Women*. Dist. by Rizzoli, 1987.

Field, Richard S. *Recent American Etching*. Middletown, Conn.: Davison Art Center, 1975.

Fine, Ruth E. *The 1980's: Prints from the Collection of Joshua P. Smith*. Washington National Gallery of Art, 1989.

Haslem, Jane. *The Innovators: Renaissance in American Printmaking*. Washington, D.C.: Haslem Fine Arts, 1973.

Johnson, Una E. *Ten Years of American Prints: 1947- 1956*. New York: Brooklyn Museum, 1956.

Smith, Selma. *Printworld Directory of Contemporary Prints and Prices, 1988-1989*. Printworld, 1988.

Tancock, John L. *Multiples — The First Decade*. Philadelphia: Philadelphia Museum of Art, 1971.

PRINT COLLECTING

Brown, J.H.V. *A Guide to Collecting Fine Prints*, Metuchen, NJ: Scarecrow Press, 1989

Calloway, Stephen. *English Prints for the Collector*. Overlook Press, 1981.

Donson, Theodore B. *Prints and the Print Market*. New York: T.Y. Crowell, 1977.

Foster, Donald L. *Prints in the Public Library*. Metuchen (N.J.): Scarecrow Press, 1973.

Gilmour, Pat. *Artists in Print: An Introduction to Prints & Printmaking*. Parkwest Publications, 1984.

Hayden, Arthur, and Blunt, Cyril G.E. *Chats on Old Prints*. London, Benn, 1957.

Hughes, Therle. *Prints for the Collector: British Prints from 1500 to 1900)*. New York: Praeger, 1971.

Rosenwald, Lessing G. *Recollections of a Collector*. Jenkintown (Pa.): The Alverthorpe Gallery, 1976.

Salamon, Fernando. *A Collector's Guide to Prints and Printmakers from Durer to Picasso*. New York: American Heritage Press, 1972.

Shapiro, Cecile, and Mason, Lauris. *Fine Prints: Collecting, Buying & Selling*. New York: Harper & Row, 1976.

Simons, Rosemary. *Collecting Original Prints*. The Christies International Collectors Series: Mayflower Books. Smith Publishers, 1980.

Weitenkampf, Frank. *The Quest of the Print*. New York: Charles Scribner's Sons, 1932.

Zigrosser, Carl and Gaedhe, Christa M. *A Guide to the Collecting and Care of Original Prints*. New York: Crown Publishers, 1965.

PRINTMAKING

Alexander, Dorothy & Strauss, Walter L. *The German Single-Leaf Woodcut, 1600-1700*. 2 Volumes. Abaris Books, 1978.

Antreasian, Garo Z., and Adams, Clinton. *The Tamarind Book of Lithography: Art and Techniques.* New York: Harry N. Abrams, 1971.

Arnold, Grant. *Creative Lithography & How to Do It.* Dover, 1941.

Biggs, John R. *Classic Woodcut Art & Engraving: An International Collection & Practical Handbook.* England: Blandford Press, 1988.

Brunner, Felix A. *A Handbook of Graphic Reproductive Processes.* New York: Hastings House, 1962. 3rd ed., 1968.

Chatto, William A. *Treatise on Wood Engraving, Historical and Practical.* Gale, 1969.

Clark, Alvin L., Jr. *From Mannerism to Classicism: Printmaking in France, 1600-1660.* Baier, Lesley K., and Kenney, Elise K., eds. Yale Art Gallery, 1987.

Clemson, Katie, and Simmons, Rosemary. *The Complete Manual of Relief Printmaking.* Knopf, 1988.

Daniels, Harvey. *Printmaking.* New York: Viking Press, 1971.

Eichenberg, Fritz. *Lithography & Silkscreen - Art and Technique.* Apollo.

Field, Richard S., and Sperling, Louise. *Offset Lithography.* Middletown (Conn.): Davison Art Center, 1973.

Gilmour, Pt. *Lasting Impressions: Lithography as Art.* University of Pennsylvania Press, 1988.

Goldman, Judith. *American Prints: Process & Proofs.* Icon Editions Series. Harper Row, 1982.

Griffiths, Antony. *Prints & Printmaking: An Introduction to the History & Techniques.* Knopf, 1981.

Heller, Jules. *Printmaking Today: A Studio Handbook.* New York: Holt, Rinehart & Winston, 1972.

Hitchings, Sinclair. *The Flowering of American Printmaking.* Amon Carter Museum: U.of Texas Press, 1988.

Ivins, William M., Jr. *Prints & Books.* Da Capa, 1969.

Lehmann-Haupt, Hellmut. *An Introduction to the Woodcut of the Seventeenth Century.* Abaris Books, 1978.

Linton, W.J. *The History of Wood-Engraving in America.* Longwood Publications Group, 1977. Reproduction of 1882 edition library binding.

Peterdi, Gabor. *Printmaking Methods Old and New.* New York: Macmillan Company, 1971.

Rhein, Erich. *The Art of Print Making.* New York: Van Nostrand Reinhold Co., 1966. Ravensburg (German): Otto Maier Verlag, 1956.

Ross, John, and Romano, Clare. *The Complete Printmaker.* New York: Free Press (Macmillan Company), 1972.

Rothenstein, Michael. *Relief Printing.* New York: Watson-Guptill Publications, 1970.

Rumpel, Heinrich. *Wood Engraving.* Geneva: Editions de Bonvent, 1973.

Russ, Stephen. *A complete Guide to Printmaking.* New York: Viking Press, 1975.

Sopher, Marcus S., and Lazzaro-Bruno, Claudia. *Sixteenth-Century Italian Prints.* Galleries Coll., 1978.

Strauss, Walter L. *The German Single-Leaf Woodcut, 1550- 1600.* Abaris Books, 1976.

Tatham, David. *Prints & Printmakers of New York State, 1825-1940.* New York State Studies: Syracuse University Press, 1986.

Wallen, Burr, and Stein, Donna. *The Cubist Print.* University of Washington Press, 1981.

PRINT CONNOISSEURSHIP

Arnau, Frank. *Art of the Faker.* Boston: Little, Brown & Co., 1961.

Castleman, Riva. *Printed Art: A View of Two Decades.* Museum of Modern Art, 1979.

Churchill, W.A. *Watermarks in the XVII and XVIII Centuries.* Amsterdam, 1935. Reprint. Amsterdam: Menno Hertzberger & Co., 1965.

Druick, Douglas, and Gordon, Martin. *Buyer Beware!* New York: Martin Gordon Gallery, 1970.

Falk, Peter. *Print Price Index* (1991 Edition). Madison, Connecticut: Sound View Press, (September 1991)

Field, Richard S. *Everything you always wanted to know about prints...* Middletown (Conn.): Davison Art Center, 1973.

Gascoigne, Bamber. *How to Identify Prints: A Complete Guide to Manual and Mechanical Processes from Woodcut to Ink- Jet.* Thames Hudson, 1986.

Gordon, Martin. *Gordon's Print Price Annual, 1991.* Martin Gordon Inc., Naples, Florida,1991

Heawood, Edward. *Watermarks, Mainly of the 17th and 18th Centuries.* Hilversum, 1950. Reprint. 1969.

Hunter, Dard. *Papermaking.* New York: Alfred A. Knopf, 1967.

Ivins, William M., Jr. *How Prints Look.* Revised edition, Cohn, Marjorie B., ed. Beacon Press, 1987.

Ivins, William M., Jr. *How Prints Look.* New York: Metropolitan Museum of Art, 1943. Reprint. Boston: Beacon Press, 1968.

Journal of the Print World. 1000 Winona Road, Meredith, NH 03253. Published quarterly (by subscription only).

Kurz, Otto. *Fakes.* New Haven, 1948. Rev'd ed. New York: Dover Publications, 1967.

Mayer, E. E. *Mayer 1991 International Auction Records.* Editions Publisol, 1991

Passeron, Roger. *Impressionist Prints.* S. Konecky Associates, 1988.

Print Collector's Newsletter., 16 East 82nd Street, NY, NY 10028. Published bi-monthly (by subscription only).

Print Quarterly. 80 Carlton Hill, London NW8 0ER, England. Published quarterly. (by subscription only).

Riggs, Timothy A. *The Print Council Index to Oeuvre- Catalogues of Prints by European & American Artists.* Kraus International, 1983.

Sachs, Samuel, and Johnson, Kathryn C. *Fakes and Forgeries.* Minneapolis: Minneapolis Institute of Arts, 1973.

CARE AND CONSERVATION OF PRINTS

Barrow, W.J. *The Barrow Method of Restoring Deteriorated Documents.* Richmond, Va.: W.J. Barrow Restoration Shop, 1973.

Clapp, Anne F. *Curatorial Care of Works of Art on Paper.* N. Lyons Books, 1987.

Clapp, Anne F. *Curatorial Care of Works of Art of Paper.* Oberlin, Ohio: Intermuseum Laboratory, 2d rev. ed., 1974.

Dolloff, Francis W., and Perkinson, Roy L. *How to Care for Works of Art of Paper.* Boston: Museum of Fine Arts, 1971.

Gaehde, Christa M. *The Care and Conservation of Fine Prints* in Zigrosser, Carl, and Gaehde, Christa M. *A Guide to the Collecting and Care of Original Prints.* New York: Crown Publishers, 1966.

Glaser, Mary Todd. *Framing & Preservation of Works of Art on Paper.* New York: Parke Bernet Galleries, 1971.

Haney, W.F. *Handbook of Paper Art Conservation.* 3rd edition. Art Conservation Handbook Series: Vol. IX. Acad. Prof. Art, 1983.

PRINT DEALERS

Beginning with this third edition, dealers in original fine art prints will be allowed to run either a simple listing in this section, or a display ad up to a full page. If you are interested in a listing, or placing a display ad, please contact **Currier Publications,** 241 Main Street, Stoneham, MA 02180 (tel: (800) 344-0760) for details.

FLORIDA

American Antique Prints
Robert Wieland
33 South St. Andrew Drive
Ormond Beach, FL 32174
(904) 672-9972

(please see Display Ad)

LOUISIANA

The Forever Dear Gallery
Helen W. Hinton
6104 Line Avenue Ste. 5
Shreveport, LA 71106
(318) 868-0018

(Dealer in rare prints.)

MASSACHUSETTS

William P. Carl
P.O. Box 67178
Chestnut Hill, MA 02167
(617) 277-9135

(please see Display Ad)

Ernest S. Kramer
Fine Art & Prints
P.O. Box 37
Wellesley Hills, MA 02181
Tel: (617) 237-3635
Fax:(617) 235-0112

(please see Display Ad)

Robert Kipp
16 Wedgemere Road
Beverly, MA 01915-01435
(508) 922-6852

(please see Display Ad)

VERMONT

Steven Thomas, Inc.
Box 41 - CP
Woodstock, VT 05091
(802) 457-1764

(please see Display Ad)

WANTED TO BUY

Fine old master and modern prints by
these and other artists

Arms	Escher	Marsh
Ault	Geerlings	Matisse
Avery	Goya	Matulka
Bacon	Haden	Meryon
Barker	Hartley	Millet
Baumann	Hassam	Moran
Bellows	Hayter	Munch
Benson	Heckel	Nason
Benton	Homer	Nordfeldt
Besnard	Hopkins	Pascin
Bone	Hopper	Patterson
Bonnard	Hunt	Pennell
Buhot	Kent	Picasso
Burchfield	Kirchner	Rembrandt
Burr	Kollwitz	Riggs
Cassatt	Kuniyoshi	Schanker
Chamberlain	Landacre	Sheeler
Coleman	Landeck	Sloan
Cook	Lazzell	Tissot
Corot	Lewis	Toulouse-Lautrec
Curry	Lozowick	Wengenroth
Davis	McBey	Whistler
Durer	Manet	Wood
Duveneck	Marin	Zorn

WILLIAM P. CARL
Post Office Box 67178
Chestnut Hill, MA 02167

(617) 277-9135

Antique Print Restoration
serving the entire country

Prints ~ Drawings ~ Watercolors

CONSERVATION AND RESTORATION

For the past fifteen years we have specialized in the conservation and restoration of Currier and Ives prints. Our cleaning and restoration process neither harms the paper fibers nor the original hand coloring. For free estimates and more information on our restoration services, please call or write.

• Request our price list for hand-crafted Birds Eye Maple frames •

508 • 922 • 6852
Robert P. Kipp

16 Wedgemere Road Beverly, Massachusetts 01945 - 1435

AUCTION HOUSES

Here is a list, worldwide, of those auction houses which sell a large volume of fine art prints each year. A good number have in-house print specialists who do the research on each consignment and see that it is properly catalogued.

Please keep in mind, most *major* auction houses today will not accept a single consignment unless it is valued at over $500. With prints you may find that the auction house will often suggest combining two or more prints together to make a "lot." Check the policies of each, when you initially contact them. In general, the commission rate charged the consignor will fall between 6% and 20%. The more valuable your piece, the lower the commission should be.

Kvaliten Auktionsverkeet
A B Stockholms Auktionsverk
Jacobgatan 10, Box 16356
103 25 Stockholm, Sweden
Tel# 08-14-24-40
Fax# 08-10-28-45

James R. Bakker Antiques Inc
370 Broadway
Cambridge, MA 02139
Tel# 617-864-7067

Galerie Gerda Bassenge
Erdener Strasse 5A
1000 Berlin 33, Germany
Tel# 030-8-92-90-13
Fax# 030-8-91-80-25

Bonhams
Montpelier Street
Knightsbridge
London SW7 1HH, England
Tel# 071-584-9161
Fax# 071-589-4072

Frank H. Boos Gallery
420 Enterprise Court
Bloomfield Hills, MI 48013
Tel# 313-332-1500
Fax# 313-332-6370

Butterfield & Butterfield
220 San Bruno Avenue
San Francisco, CA 94103
Tel# 415-861-7500
Fax# 415-861-8951

Christie's East
219 East 67th St
New York, NY 10021
Tel# 212-606-0400
Fax# 212-737-6076

Christie, Manson & Woods,
London
8 King St., St.James
London SW1Y 6QT, England
Tel# 071-839-9060
Fax# 071-839-1611

Christie, Manson & Woods,
New York
502 Park Ave
New York, NY 10022
Tel# 212-546-1000
Fax# 212-980-8163

Christie's South Kensington
85 Old Brompton Rd
London SW7 3JS, England
Tel# 071-581-7611
Fax# 071-584-0431

Bruce Collins
Seaboard Auction Gallery
Rte. 236 North
Eliot, ME
Tel# 207-452-2197

F. Dorling Buch Und
Kunstantiquariat
Neur Wall 40-42
2000 Hamburg 36, Germany
Tel# 040-36-67-07
Fax# 040-36-23-58

Dorotheum Kunstabteilung
Dorothegasse 17
1010 Vienna, Austria
Tel# 01-515-60-0
Fax# 01-515-60-443

William Doyle Galleries
175 East 87th St
New York, NY 10028
Tel# 212-427-2370
Fax# 212-369-0892

Hotel Druout
9, rue Druout
75009 paris, France
Tel# 14-246 17 11

Du Mouchelle Art Galleries
409 East Jefferson Ave
Detroit, MI 48226
Tel# 313-963-0248
Fax# 313-963-8199

Eberhart Auktionen
Seestrasse 13
8702 Zollikon 2, Switzerland
Tel# 01-392-02-30
Fax# 01 392-01-86

Robert C. Eldred Co., Inc.
Route 6A
East Dennis, MA 02641
Tel# 508-385-3116
Fax# 508-385-7201

Galerie Fischer
Haldenstrasse 19
CH-6006 Luzern, Switzerland
Tel# 041-51 57 72

Villa Grisbach
Fasanenstrasse 25
D-1000 Berlin 15, Germany
Tel# 030-882 68 11
Fax# 030-882 41 45

Grogan & Company
890 Commonwealth Ave.
Boston, MA 02215
Tel# 617-566-4100
Fax# 617-566-7715

Hartung & Hartung
Karolinenplatz 5A
D 8000 Munich 2, Germany
Tel# 089-28-40-34

Hauswedell & Nolte
Poseldorfer Weg 1
2000 Hamburg 13, Germany
Tel# 040-44-83-86
Fax# 040-4-10-41-98

Leslie Hindman
215 West Ohio
Chicago, IL 60610
Tel# 312-670-0100
Fax# 312-670-4248

Karl & Faber
Amirplatz 3
8000 Munich 2, Germany
Tel# 089-2-28-33-50

Galerie Wolfgang Ketterer
Brienner Strasse 25
8000 Munich 2, Germany
Tel# 089-59-11-81
Fax# 089-59-62-19

Galerie Koller
Ramistrasse 8
8024 Zurich, Switzerland
Tel# 01-47-50-40
Fax# 01-26-19-60-8

Galerie Kornfeld
Laupenstrasse 41
Bern, Switzerland
Tel# 41-31-26-46-73
Fax# 41-31-26-18-91

Kunsthallen
Kobmagergade 11
1150 Copenhagen K, Denmark
Tel# 33-13-85-69
Fax# 33-32-46-70

Kunsthaus Lempertz
Neumarkt 3
5000 Cologne 1, Germany
Tel# 0221-23-68-67
Fax# 0221-23-68-167

Litchfield Auction Gallery
Box 1337, Rte. 202
Litchfield, CT 06759
Tel# 203-567-3126

Neumeister Kunstauktionhaus
Barer Strasse 37
8000 Munich 40, Germany
Tel# 089-28-17-10-0
Fax# 089-23-17-10-55

Phillips, Son & Neale
11 New Bond Street
London W1Y 0AS, England
Tel# 01-629-6602
Fax# 01-629-8876

Poster Auctions International
37 Riverside Dr
New York, NY 10023
Tel# 212-787-4000
Fax# 212-877-2347

Arne Bruun Rasmussen
Bregade 33
1260 Copenhagen K, Denmark
Tel# 33-13-69-11
Fax# 33-32-49-20

Robert K. Skinner
2 Newbury St
Boston, MA 02116
Tel# 617-236-1700

Sotheby's, London
34 & 35 New Bond St
London W1A 2AA, England
Tel# 01-493-8080
Fax# 071-409-3100

Sotheby's, New York
1334 York Ave
New York, NY 10021
Tel# 212-606-7000
Fax# 212-606-7107

Swann Galleries
104 East 25th St
New York, NY 10010
Tel# 212-254-4710
Fax# 212-979-1017

Galerie Henner Wachholtz
Mittelweg 43
2000 Hamburg 13, Germany
Tel# 040-44-04-14

Waverly Auctions
4931 Cordell Ave, Ste AA
Bethesda, MD 20814
Tel# 301-951-8883

Weschler's
905 E Street NW
Washington, DC 20004
Tel# 202-628-1282
Fax# 202-628-2366

Winter Associates
21 Cooke St, Box 823
Plainville, CT 06062
Tel# 203-793-0288

Arno Winterberg
Blumenstrasse 15
6900 Heidelberg 1, Germany
Tel# 06-221-22-631
Fax# 06-221-164631

Wolf's Auction Gallery
1239 West 6th Street
Cleveland, OH 44113
Tel# 216-575-9653

INSTITUTIONS

The following list is a compilation of those institutions, nationally, which house large collections of prints and are great resources for research. Many have extensive libraries as well as immense collections of fine art prints.

Achenbach Foundation for
    Graphic Arts
California Palace of the
    Leigon of Honor Museum
Lincoln Park
San Francisco, CA 94121

Addison Gallery of Amer. Art
Phillips Academy
Andover, MA 01810

Albright Knox Art Gallery
1285 Elmwood Ave
Buffalo, NY 14222

Allen Memorial Art Museum
OBerlin College
Oberlin, OH 44074

Alvethorpe Gallery
Lessing J.Rosenwald Collection
511 Meetinghouse Rd
Jenkintown, PA 19046

Art Institute of Chicago
Michigan and Adams
Chicago, IL 60611

Baltimore Museum of Art
Art Museum Dr
Baltimore, MD 21218

William Benton Museum of Art
University of Connecticut
Storrs, CT 06226

Boston Athenaeum
10 1/2 Beacon St
Boston, MA 02108
617-227-0270

Boston Public Library
Print Department
Dartmouth St
Boston, MA 02117

Brooklyn Museum
188 Eastern Pkwy
Brooklyn, NY 11238

Busch-Reisinger Museum
29 Kirkland St
Cambridge, MA 02138

Cincinnati Art Museum
Department of Prints
Eden Park
Cincinnati, OH 45202

Sterling & Francine Clark
Art Institute
South St
Williamstown, MA 01267

Cleveland Museum of Art
11150 East Blvd
Cleveland, OH 44106

Colonial Williamsburg Found.
Department of Collections
Williamsburg, VA 23185

Cooper-Hewitt Museum of
Design
9 East 90th St
New York, NY 10028

Davison Art Center
301 High St
Wesleyan University
Middletown, CT 06457

Detroit Institute of Arts
Dept. of Graphic Arts
5200 Woodward Ave
Detroit, MI 48202

Fogg Art Museum
Dept. of Prints & Photographs
Harvard University
Cambridge, MA 02138

Free Library of Philadelphia
Print & Picture Dept
Logan Sq
Philadelphia, PA 19103

The Frick Collection
1 East 70th St
New York, NY 10021

Grolier Club Library
47 East 60th ST
New York, NY 10022

Grunwald Center for the
Graphic Arts
Univ. of Cal., Los Angeles
405 Hilgard Ave
Los Angeles, CA 90024

Solomon R. Guggenheim
Museum
1071 Fifth Ave
New York, NY 10028

Herbert I. Johnson
Museum of Art
Cornell University
Ithaca, NY 14853

High Museum of Art
1280 Peachtree St NE
Atlanta, GA 30309

Hispanic Society of America
Broadway & 155 St
New York, NY 10032

Houghton Library
Harvard University
Dept. of Printing & Graphic
Arts
Cambridge, MA 02138

Henry E. Huntington Library
Art Gallery & Botanical
Gardens
1151 Oxford Rd
San Marino, CA 91108

Kimbell Art Museum
P.O. Box 9440
Will Rogers Road West
Fort Worth, TX 76107

Library of Congress
Prints & Photographs Div.
2nd St. & Independence Ave SE
Washington, DC 20540

Los Angeles County Museum
of Art
5905 Wilshire Blvd
Los Angeles, CA 90036

Madison Art Center
720 East Gorham
Madison, WS 53703

Metropolitan Museum of Art
Dept. of Prints&Photographs
Fifth Ave at 82nd St
New York, NY 10025

Minneapolis Inst. of Art
Dept. of Prints & Dwgs
2400 Third Ave S.
Minneapolis, MN 55404

Pierpont Morgan Library
29 East 36th St
New York, NY 10016

Munson-Williams-Proctor
Institute
310 Genesee St
Utica, NY 13502

Museum of Fine Arts
479 Huntington Ave
Boston, MA 02115

Museum of Fine Arts-Houston
1001 Bissonnet
Houston, TX 77005

Museum of Modern Art
11 West 53rd St
New York, NY 10019

Nat'nl Museum of American Art
Smithsonian Institution
Ninth & G St., NW
Washington, DC 20560

National Gallery of Art
Sixth St. & Constitution
Ave, NW
Washington, DC 20565

Nelson Gallery-Atkins Museum
4525 Oak St
Kansas City, MO 64111

New York Historical Society
Print Room
170 Central Park West
New York, NY 10024

New York Public Library
Prints Divison
Fifth Ave & 42nd St
New York, NY 10018

Philadelphia Museum of Art
Benjamin Franklin Pkwy
@ 26th St
Philadelphia, PA 19101

Picker Art Gallery
Colgate University
Hamilton, NY 13346

Portland Museum of Art
1219 S.W. Park
Portland, OR 97205

Princeton Univ. Art Museum
Print Room
Princeton, NJ 18540

Rhode Island School of Design
Museum of Art
224 Benefit St
Providence, RI 02903

St. Louis Art Museum
Forest Park
St. Louis, MO 63110

San Francisco Museum of Art
Van Ness Ave @ McAllister St
San Francisco, CA 94102

Smith College Museum of Art
Northampton, MA 01060

Toledo Museum of Art
Toledo, OH 43697

Wadsworth Atheneum
Hartford, CT 06115

Walker Art Center
Vineland Pl
Minneapolis, MN 55403

Whitney Museum of
American Art
945 Madison Ave
New York, NY 10021

Henry Francis de Pont
Winterthur Museum
Winterthur, DE 19735

Worcester Art Museum
j55 Salisbury St
Worcester, MA 01608

Yale Univ Art Gallery
1111 Chapel St
New Haven, CT 06520

Important Notes

Important Notes